WITHDRAWN

ALSO BY ROBERT M. HOCHHEISER

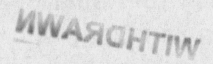

IT'S A JOB, NOT A JAIL

How to Break Your Shackles When You Can't Afford to Quit

ROBERT M. HOCHHEISER

A FIRESIDE BOOK
Published by Simon & Schuster

F

FIRESIDE
Rockefeller Center
1230 Avenue of the Americas
New York, NY 10020

Fireside and colophon are registered trademarks
of Simon & Schuster Inc.

Designed by Irving Perkins Associates, Inc.

Manufactured in the United States of America

1   3   5   7   9   10   8   6   4   2

Library of Congress Cataloging-in-Publication Data
Hochheiser, Robert M., date.
It's a job, not a jail : how to break your shackles
when you can't afford to quit / Robert M. Hochheiser
p. cm.
1. Career plateaus. 2. Career changes. 3. Job stress 4. Work—
Psychological aspects. 5. Psychology, Industrial. I. Title.
HF5384.5.H63   1998
650.14—dc21   97-41766 CIP
ISBN 0-684-80458-1

4/98

.......Contents.......

..AUTHOR'S NOTE..

Impossible bosses may bear no resemblance whatsoever to human beings, but my purpose here is to provide career advice, not to ridicule, embarrass, or defame anyone. Neither do I want my words rewritten by a bunch of lawyers. I have therefore chosen names, circumstances, and descriptions in such a way that any resemblance between real people and those portrayed in this book is purely coincidental. Likewise for companies.

This is not at its essence, however, a work of fiction. You will read many anecdotes on the following pages. I have not dreamt them up. The situations they represent are completely true, as are the lessons you can learn from them. The rest is up to you.

1

The Six Keys to Job Satisfaction

Okay, you're good at what you do, really good—perhaps the best. But that isn't worth anything to you right now. Your job, to use the current vernacular, sucks. If you feel that way because you're subjected to sexual harassment, physical abuse, or other treatment that puts you in danger, stop reading right here. Stand up, grab your coat, and get out. *Now.* No job is worth losing your life, your health, or your personal integrity.

If your job is intolerable without being imminently unsafe, however, keep on reading. Perhaps the boss is hard to get along with, the politics are unbearable, or the working conditions atrocious. Maybe what you are doing is boring, too limited, or not well-paying enough. Whatever your grounds, you hate your job and you want nothing more than to leave it.

You've looked and looked for employment elsewhere, but with no success. The economy is terrible and only a few people are hiring. Half of them are paying nickel-and-dime wages, while the other half are located in places where you wouldn't want to live or work. Either that or you sense that they would bury you under the same kind of nonsense that's stinking up your current job. As much as you hate to admit it, nothing's out there for you at the moment.

Unless they have generous uncles who croak and leave them a ton of cash, most people struggling in terrible jobs do nothing except tough it out until they can land something better. But I'm going to offer you another choice: a way to turn a job you hate into one that treats you nicely.

I'll start by pointing out something that you may have noticed on your own; you are not a kangaroo. A jackass, perhaps, and maybe even a baboon or an economist, but not a kangaroo. I know something about these marsupials, because I used to behave like one of them. Unfortunately, however, neither my knees nor my feet were strong enough for heavy-duty jumping, and my tail provided more ballast than balance. The more I hopped about, the more I tripped over my own feet, ran into obstacles, or landed in something that neither smelled nice nor provided good traction.

You're missing my point if you think I speak literally and only about walking. If all his or her parts are intact and functioning, any idiot can walk. Instead of bouncing all over creation, the trick to increasing job satisfaction is to proceed in a generally forward direction; learning and improving as we go. Rather than hopping from place to place throughout the early stages of my career, I would have been a lot better off if I had moved one foot at a time, one step at a time, one right after the other.

"Gradual progression" is not a difficult concept to understand. Small children master it all the time, and occasionally even some congressmen have been known to figure it out. Not me. For most of my career, I went to work day after day without ever looking at consequences, never putting my actions in the perspective of an overall career plan, and never thinking much beyond tomorrow.

It took me years to wise up to how and why things happen in the world of working people. "It's bad enough I have to work for a living," I used to tell myself. "But no amount of money would be enough to justify the crap I put up with on this job." Sound familiar? You've probably felt that way once or twice in your career. A lot of people do. I always did. In my view, every job was horrible, and I came to look on good jobs as being like blue bananas—nonexistent. "If 'good job' is an oxymoron," I reasoned further, "I must be a moron for working here."

I was a moron, all right. Not for working where I worked, but for blaming all my problems on others and for taking too long to learn from my mistakes. I finally did figure things out, however, and now I can help you do the same.

For the first eleven years of my career, I moved steadily up the corporate ladder. Then I hit a fourteen-year stretch during which I had five jobs, none of which lasted long. I was fired from three of those jobs, laid off from another when the company went out of business, and left one voluntarily.

At the first company that tossed me out, I had been sales and marketing VP for three years during which profits doubled and sales tripled. I had no fights or disagreements of any kind with the boss. He sent nothing but compliments, raises, and bonuses my way until he called me into his office one day and gave me an hour to clear out and get lost. *Why?* I asked. But all he said was that I wasn't "panning out" to his satisfaction.

That bastard! All I could think of was the cast-iron frying pan at home. If I had it at work, I might have been tempted to redistribute his facial features with it. To say that I was stunned and hurt would be the understatement of the age.

I was out of work for three months before I hooked up with a small company on the verge of folding. I helped them enter a new market, which increased their business tenfold in a year and a half. The firm grew so big that it had to move to larger quarters. Guess who didn't go with them? I got the boot just before the new plant opened.

At that point, I proceeded in a fashion best described as just plain stupid. I was sure that my career would still be on the upswing had I not had the bad luck to run up against a string of evildoers who were totally at fault for my predicament.

Who were these scoundrels? The bosses who fired me were at the top of my list, followed closely by those who succeeded me. I imagined that others were so jealous of my talents that they lied to force me out. How easy it was to divert blame. Scapegoating felt good, but it never added a dime to my income. Neither did it even once help me to get a new job. I was so into feeling sorry for myself that I was unable to detect the real villain who wrecked my career: me. I had to change my thinking before I could change the direction in which my career was heading.

But I didn't have the time for thinking just then. I was too busy playing kangaroo. Instead of thinking, I jumped from situation to situation, looking narrowly at each as if it had no meaning past the isolated circumstances in which it occurred. The following examples will explain what I mean.

LISTENING

As the chief engineer for a company in Cincinnati some years ago, I was also the youngest vice president, the darling of the executive board, and the rising star corporate insiders looked upon as the person most likely to succeed the current CEO. So much for their insight and wisdom. I traveled a great deal back then, and one day I took a flight from Los Angeles to Kansas City.

When the plane reached cruising altitude, I opened up my briefcase, pulled out several notebooks, and set about finishing a report I was working on. I was buried in papers, but that obviously didn't matter to the tall young woman in the next seat. She started to talk as soon as I sat down, and she never stopped.

She was going back home and quite apprehensive about meeting her ex-husband. "We were married at seventeen," she went on to say, "but I divorced him after two years." She called an end to the marriage because he was prone to violence and beat her up several times. Not satisfied with leaving him, she left her job, left town, and moved to California, where she became a court stenographer. That was three years earlier.

On and on she went, telling me how much she liked the West Coast, her job, and an Air Force lieutenant she had started dating. But, she still had strong feelings for her former husband. He had gone to counseling, he swore that his problems were behind him, and she agreed to return to see for herself.

"Why am I being given this information?" I asked myself. I didn't care about her little soap opera. I had work to do, and I had counted on being able to do it on that flight. Yet I couldn't shut her up, and I didn't want to be rude. So I tried to work, acting as if I were listening, and gesturing as if I were interested.

As we deplaned, I saw her plant a big wet one on the lips of an obviously nervous young man carrying a gigantic bouquet of flowers. But I didn't hang around; I went to my hotel room to write my report. Doing that, however, turned out to be much easier than satisfying my curiosity about why a total stranger was telling me all these personal details.

My wife explained it to me when I got home. The woman told me her story because she had a need to express herself, to let someone know what was on her mind. She couldn't bottle it up, and as a total stranger, I was the perfect one on whom to vent her feelings. I told her that I lived and worked thousands of miles away. Even if I were to repeat what she said to all my friends, it would never get back to her, the people she knew in Missouri and California, the lieutenant she had met, or the man who wanted to win her back.

I'd love to tell you the rest of the story, but I don't know any more. I never even got the woman's name. All I know is that she had a need to share her problems. We all have such a need, but I didn't see that at the time, so for years I never took advantage of it—particularly in the way I conducted myself at work.

BUILDING TRUST

Another experience I misread years ago took place when I was sales manager for a New York City company. One day our sales rep in North Carolina, Tom Poole, called me with some incredible news. After pursuing a potentially big customer in Greensboro for several months, Tom told me that we could close a sizable order if I were to visit the customer and personally assure him that we could meet his specifications.

I was on the first plane to Greensboro the next morning, and Tom took me right to that customer, a tank of a man named Fred. Genial and brandishing the thickest possible backwoods accent, Fred ushered us into his office, offered us seats, and started to talk, but not about business.

After we discussed the weather, Fred asked Tom what he thought about their mayor. I'd never heard of their mayor, but they talked about him anyway, proceeding from there to discuss everything from the previous week's football games to the pros and cons of various local hunting and fishing sites. I knew nothing about these topics and cared even less. Not wanting to seem like an idiot or a useless appendage, I laughed when they laughed and nodded approvingly at the right times. I also jumped in whenever I could add to what they were saying, but that didn't happen much.

You can't begin to imagine my surprise when, after about forty minutes, Fred excused himself to go to a meeting, and thanked me for coming to see him on such short notice. I wish I could have seen the look on my face. Our meeting was apparently over, and we hadn't said word one about the million dollar order I was expecting. I didn't know what to do or say, but Tom did.

"By the way, Fred, did you get a chance to look at our proposal?" I had traveled hundreds of miles to close the sale of the year, and the best Tom could do in the way of a sales pitch was *"By the way"*? I could have strangled him, but Fred's answer interrupted my train of thought. "Oh sure, Tom. It looked good to me. I signed the purchase order when I came in this morning. Mary Jo can give you a copy on your way out."

Fred had approved the paperwork before he even met me, so why did he insist on my coming down to see him if he was going to give us the sale anyway? That was the question I hit Tom with when we got back to his car. He laughed, and then he apologized, explaining that Fred knew that our product was good, but he didn't know whether *I* was any good. He asked me down to size me up. I was the guy he would have to call if he had problems down the road. Little did I know that just by making the effort to visit Fred on his own turf, I had already won half the battle. The other half was won by walking through his door and not being a jerk. Had I had given the impression that their small talk was stupid or meaningless as I thought it was, we might never have clinched the deal.

Fred didn't want to do business with a company. To him, a company was a thing, and he wasn't comfortable unless he could deal with people he sensed he could trust. He may not at that point have trusted me with his life, but he probably did think he could trust me to show up if he had a problem, and to treat him in a reasonable manner. As soon as he felt that he had what he wanted, he gave me what I wanted. It was that simple.

WAKING UP

Things didn't start turning around for me until I lost my fourth job in eleven years. My unemployment benefits ran out six months later, and just when life seemed as dark as I'd ever seen it, a speck of light intruded on my gloom.

A headhunter who previously said he had nothing for me called to say that one of his clients might need me, not as an employee, but as a freelance writer for one specific assignment that could be completed in about three weeks. "It's better than nothing," I told myself. So, I met the client. His name was Charlie Greene, and he hired me.

The work did take only a few weeks, but Charlie liked what I did and he asked me to take on a second project. When that was done, he gave me a third assignment, and then a string of others. All of a sudden and much to my surprise, I had become self-employed as a consultant in technical writing and corporate public relations.

Charlie asked that I meet him once a week to update him on the progress of my work, and I suggested we do that over lunch on Mondays. He accepted, and for months afterward, we got together at noon on the first day of virtually every week.

During the first few of those lunches, all we talked about was the work he asked me to do for him. As time went on, however, other matters crept into our conversations. Every time I went to see the man, we'd meet for close to two hours—thirty minutes in his office, an hour or so at lunch, and another half hour back at the office. Maybe fifteen minutes of all that was on business. The rest of the time we'd discuss other matters; the problems Charlie faced on a daily basis, inside dirt on various luminaries at the company, and war stories from the places where he used to work. He told me about his wife's job, his daughter's new car, and his son's divorce.

Why was he inundating me with all this stuff about his personal life? I didn't ask for it. The answer dawned on me when I realized that he had a lot in common with that young woman I had met on an airplane years earlier. Their lives and lifestyles were worlds apart, yet they were both giving me information—not because I wanted it, because they had a basic human need to talk about it. All I had to do was listen, offer advice only when asked for it, and not be judgmental.

I was not accustomed to having someone bare his soul to me like that. The people I used to work with never opened up to me like that and neither did many of my friends. As someone who got paid by the hour, however, I really didn't mind listening to Charlie. In fact, I had no choice but to listen. Since he was my only source of income, I couldn't afford to antagonize him. As far as I was concerned, he could yak all he liked, I'd bill him for the time, and we'd both be happy.

I remember reminding myself of that one day when it hit me that every boss I ever had was my only source of income. I had never looked at them in that light. Maybe they didn't talk to me because I never seemed inclined to listen to what they had to say. Perhaps if I *had* listened, I would have been in a better position to understand what I would have had to do to please them.

The importance of listening had occurred to me out of the blue. I was intrigued, but not yet convinced that listening could solve my problems. It seemed too simple. To investigate further, I steered my conversations with other customers away from business and toward their interests as persons with lives outside of their work. It wasn't hard; I just asked a few nonprobing questions about their families, school ties, hobbies, and so forth.

This strategy didn't work on everybody. A few of my customers had no reaction, and I wasn't exactly an expert at getting people to open up and talk with me, so I didn't press. But two or three others did warm up and send assignments my way.

Then I got a call from Steve Marks, a former boss. Hearing from Steve was a surprise since, to the best of my knowledge, my hatred of him was matched only by his disgust with me. Dictatorial and highly self-centered, Steve couldn't bring himself to delegate authority, while I was stubborn, uncompromising, and unwilling to tolerate his telling me how to do my job. We fought constantly for the three years I was in his employ, and he eventually fired me.

Memories of working for Steve began flooding back the minute he called. I couldn't imagine why he wanted to talk, but he had a big project to do, and no one to do it in-house.

He heard that I had become a wordslinger for hire and he was willing to pay for my services. That's why he asked me to come in, and that's why I complied willingly with his wishes. I was a struggling entrepreneur in search of a buck wherever I could find it. None of this had anything to do with liking each other; it was business.

By then, however, I finally understood the true significance of my experience with Fred from Greensboro, and I could see parallels with every boss I ever had, not just Steve. Instead of trying so damn hard to impress people with the quality of my work and the brilliance of my ideas, I should have paid more attention to getting them to feel safe with me and trust me.

Each of those bosses had an agenda—a set of personal goals. I assumed that I wanted what they wanted, but that assumption was way out in left field. Steve's interests and mine were in total conflict: he wanted control, and I wanted to be left alone. Other bosses may have had other needs, but my relationships were pretty much the same with each of them. One of us was oil, the other was water, and never the twain would blend.

I had no concern for their needs. My only concern was with doing a good job, but they didn't know that. They knew only what they thought they saw in me: a person who was headstrong, looking to make a name for himself, and possibly a threat who was out to take their jobs, their profits, or both.

A threat? Yes. They probably felt threatened by my annoyance at having to get their approval on everything I did. The custom in most companies is to consult with the boss before proceeding on a task, but I had a different custom. I did things on my own initiative. Nothing I did went wrong, but my bosses were frightened nonetheless that I might rock too many boats and put them or their companies in jeopardy. Several of them eventually replaced me with people they did trust.

I can't blame them for that. Looking back now, I blame myself for poorly conveying my intentions. I didn't want any of their power; I wanted only to do my work and to be recognized for doing it well.

But that was in the past. When Steve called, all I could think of was avoiding the battles we used to have. So, I immediately asked him how his wife and daughter were. As much as I despised him, I liked them. He did too, and discussing them obviously made him feel relaxed and less inclined to talk about himself than usual. He talked about several topics, I listened, I billed him for the time, and he paid. You had better believe he paid.

As with all my clients, I did the best I could for Steve. This included giving advice, but I didn't push it and I didn't care if he followed my counsel. I still couldn't stand the man on a personal level, but that became irrelevant. The company was his toy, and he was paying the freight, so to speak. As long as he gave me the business I wanted, I was happy to let him be as right or as wrong as he wanted.

MYTHS VS. REALITIES

Like everyone else in our society, you have probably been bombarded from birth with the notion that to get, keep, and grow in a job, you have to be willing and able to perform that job to perfection.

This sounds good, but it's nothing more than a half-truth; a view of life more mythical than it is realistic. Being *willing* means hard work, dedication, and loyalty to the job, but how about *able?* Conventional wisdom tells us that being able means having enough skills and education to do specific job tasks. Not only is this what we're taught in school, it's also the basis on which all job training programs are designed.

Of course you need skill and know-how to get a good job. I'm not disputing that. But I *am* challenging the premise that you can get any job you want and rise to any level you want merely by doing your work better than anyone else. This is simply false. Your engineering, accounting, marketing, or artistic abilities will take you only so far. Beyond that, they're useless. That I discovered the hard way. My career didn't sour because I suddenly forgot how to do my work. It soured because I ran into the stone wall called human nature.

No matter how well you can do something, regardless of how long you have done it, or how good your credentials are, you can't hire yourself to work for a company you don't own. Someone has to do that for you. Accordingly, you have a good shot at a job only if you are adept at convincing another person to hire you.

If you are inept as an interviewer, you may lose out to another applicant whose only talent is interviewing. Likewise for keeping a job and benefiting from it. Without someone else, you'd never get a raise, a promotion, or access to the assistance and favors you need every now and again.

You can't even work for yourself alone. You'll soon go under if someone else doesn't buy whatever you are selling. I'm a writer, but I need an army of someone elses: customers, office suppliers, computer manufacturers, and many others, including readers. I may be in business *for* myself, but I could not stay in business *by* myself.

Another myth we've been brought up to believe is that the workplace is an environment in which people pull together to meet common goals. That's the way it should be, but rarely is. Many bosses think only of themselves, their subordinates do likewise, and unless you follow suit, you may get nothing for your hard work.

The myth that makes me laugh the most is the one about "excellence in business." I'm all for excellence. Pursuing it is the smartest, most effective route to efficiency, profits, and personal fulfillment. The overwhelming majority of CEOs and other managers in our society, however, care about excellence only to the extent that they personally gain from it. No matter how much the company and its stockholders may benefit from your excellence, your boss may not want it unless he benefits as well. Give him a big enough piece of the pie and he may not care how much the company is hurt in the process.

In a perfect universe, you and I could choose from an infinite number of high-paying, interesting jobs with cooperative co-workers under the supervision of fair bosses who reward us on the basis of our demonstrated abilities and hard work. But that's wishful thinking. With rare exceptions, the real world isn't like that.

Table I lists all the major job satisfaction myths and their corresponding realities. Do not conclude from looking at Table I that the world as I see it is run entirely by greed. I merely believe that we act in our own self-interest before we act on behalf of others or of such esoteric concepts as the so-called work ethic. Self-interest rules every job and every boss; even the good ones. I'm not saying that none of them care about their work. Some care passionately, but none of them care so much that they are willing to put the job ahead of their own needs. They all put themselves first. Don't fault them for that. Putting yourself first is a survival instinct. If someone else has more of that instinct than you do, getting mad at them is not going to be the solution to your problems. Get mad at yourself.

Table I. JOB SATISFACTION MYTHS AND REALITIES

Point of Comparison	Myth	Typical Reality
You get ahead by	doing good work	doing what your bosses want you to do
You get ahead by	being a team player	thinking of yourself
Management acts in the best interests of	stockholders	themselves
Management wants you to	do good work	help them to meet their personal goals
Management wants	on-the-job excellence	excellence in filling *their* pockets
Management wants	profits and productivity	personal power and riches
Management wants	corporate growth	their own job security
Some executives are	shortsighted jerks	damn smart if their "stupidity" pays off for them
Co-workers want to	cooperate	keep you from interfering with their plans
Most people want to	be helpful	get maximum rewards for minimum work
Everybody tries to	do good work	make a good impression on the boss
Everybody tries to	do good work	look good
When things don't go right, bosses	admit their failings	look for scapegoats
The best way to get ahead is to	think only of yourself	motivate others to help you

Climbing up a hierarchic ladder demands an enormous amount of hard work and a great deal of singlemindedness in concentrating on one's own interests, sometimes to the exclusion of everything else. The most selfish people you work with are probably the people in power. Most of them will take good care of you only to the extent that they think you are helping them to meet their personal goals, *not* to the extent you help to meet the needs of the organization as a whole.

Regardless of where you work, competition is fierce for a limited number of opportunities, a finite amount of money for raises, and only so many promotions. Some highly capable people succeed, and some get only so far before falling by the wayside. We will return to the themes in Table I in the coming chapters, but for now, I'll say only that your best chance of attaining job satisfaction is to master the skills necessary to convince your bosses that you can help them to meet their personal needs better than anyone else. These are known as motivational skills or "people" skills, and they can make the difference between getting ahead and getting a headache.

DON'T JUST DO YOUR JOB, MAKE IT WORK FOR YOU

People skills are the linchpin in what I call the six keys to job satisfaction. Here's a quick rundown of what they are and how they work together.

1. **Meet your needs by meeting the needs of others.** If there is such a thing as the "secret" to success in business, this is it. The idea is to put people in your debt by making make them count on you for certain necessities in their everyday lives. The more you can get them to rely on you, the more likely they will be to treat you well.

This will not happen overnight. Using people skills goes far beyond mastering the art of perfunctory small talk. You can't perform a few small favors and expect people to go out on a limb for you. Meeting needs works only when it is done continuously and persistently.

2. **Stay focused.** You may say that you work "for" one company or another, but you must never forget that you are there for your own purposes. Do as good a job as you can, but don't be so concerned with meeting corporate goals that you lose sight of your own.

3. **Learn from your mistakes.** If things are not going well, you are doing something wrong. If you can figure out what that is and correct it, your next attempt at satisfaction may be more successful. Don't allow yourself to be hammered by the same lessons over and over again before you figure out what they mean. Instead of wasting your failures and suffering through them, treat every one as an opportunity to find something out about life and about yourself.

4. **Take charge of your career.** No one else will do this for you. Get off your gluteus maximus and go for what you want rather than waiting for it to fall into your lap. Do nothing and you will soon hate not only your job, but also yourself for allowing everybody else to control you. Instead of squandering tons of energy complaining about your job, *do* something about it.

5. **Cultivate alternative sources of satisfaction.** If you can't get satisfaction on the job, maybe you can get it "after hours"—at night and on weekends. Plan your time right and you may be able to use it to make more money, overcome new challenges, and enjoy additional forms of fulfillment.

6. **Never sacrifice or jeopardize your integrity.** The more you give to some people, the more they'll want, and the

less they'll give in return. Put a stop to that sort of non-sense and put a stop to it as soon as it starts, but be your-self. Don't try to be nasty or ruthless if that isn't what you are. The best possible you is probably a lot better than a second-rate imitation of someone else.

No, that's not all there is to job satisfaction. I wish it were, but there's more—a lot more. You've now seen an outline of *what* has to be done to get job satisfaction, so let's move on to chapter 2 and start getting more into the *how* of it.

2

Focus

Why do you stay in your current job? Is your sole purpose for working there to make money for the people who own the company? I doubt it. Is it to insure that the woman in the next office can pay her bills this month? No way. You probably have enough trouble paying your own debts, much less worrying about anyone else's.

Maybe your boss factors in to your work goals. Is your mission in life to convince the rest of the world that he's an airhead in need of a brain transplant? Or do you trudge in to work every day and put up with his crap because you are filthy rich and have nothing better to do? Somehow I think none of these "reasons" apply to you. At least I hope they don't.

ALL THE RIGHT REASONS

If gazing at the sky is your goal, you'll never reach it by burying your head in the sand. No matter what you want, you won't get it unless you have focus: the ability to keep your gaze, your thoughts, and your behavior trained precisely on getting what you want.

Taking a hike from a bad job makes no sense unless doing so leads to a better one. Yet in instance after instance, people leave job after job, hating every one of them but not knowing why. Instead of going *toward* something they want, they spend their lives taking action to *get away from* something they hate.

You work where you work only because *you* expect to get a satisfactory return on your efforts. You may have taken the job for pay, advancement, challenge, enjoyment of the work or the working conditions, but given your interest in this book, it's safe to assume that things have been less than satisfactory. For one reason or another, you hate the job, the people you work with, your bosses, or all of the above.

Table II lists many of the reasons people give for lack of job satisfaction. Look closely at the table and check any of the reasons that apply to your current situation. Differentiate between those reasons you can tolerate and those that absolutely *must* be fixed ASAP. If any one item in the table is not a problem for you, skip it and move on to the next. Add any extra reasons at the bottom.

As you fill in your answers, pay attention to your gut feelings. Table II has nothing to do with logic. If you don't like your job, you don't like it, and whether your reasons are sound is of no consequence. Job satisfaction is a matter of happiness; it's a state of mind governed by instincts and emotions, none of which may have anything in common with rational thinking.

Table II. REASONS FOR LACK OF JOB SATISFACTION

Reasons	Bad but Tolerable	Must Fix
Challenge/fulfillment		
Pressure on the job		
Enjoyable work		
Working environment		
Relationship with boss		
Relationships with others		
Freedom to act on your own		
Income		
Income growth potential		
Promotion potential		
Office politics		
Benefits (insurance, etc.)		
Job security		
Status/respect obtained		
Excitement		
Ease of commuting		

MEA CULPA

Before you start foaming at the mouth about your greedy bosses and backstabbing colleagues, look at yourself as the person who may be most responsible for your job problems. Maybe you are perceived as too selfish or pushy. Maybe your boss thinks you are trying to force him out. Such suppositions may sound ridiculous, but if people feel a certain way about you, that's a hard fact of life. They won't change their opinions about you until you change your ways of relating to them.

I'm not saying that you are the enemy, only that you should consider the possibility that you are. Each of us always has culpability in our problems at work. Even if others are responsible for your job woes, you are entirely at fault if you do nothing but complain about your bad luck and wait for the forces of righteousness to make everything nice.

Another possibility is that you are to blame for not recognizing that it's not the boss or even the job that you hate, but the type of work. Maybe you liked it when you started, but perhaps it bores you now. Perhaps you don't realize that what you need most is a new set of challenges.

In my own case, I always could have used a few dollars more, but money, as my wife will certainly confirm, has never driven me as much as it probably should have. Each time I came to hate a job, I blamed my boss, and each boss I had struck me as an absolute imbecile who went out of his way to make my life difficult. Why did I have so many bosses like that? Why were they so oppressive? Why did they make me run to them for their approval on every little decision?

I couldn't answer those questions when I was an employee, but I can now. I desperately wanted my bosses to respect me and trust me, but I refused to ask for their approval whenever I did something. When the something was small, they didn't mind, but when it was big, I frightened them. Seeing me as impetuous and headstrong, they kept the lid on me. Put in their shoes today, I might act the same way.

What hurt me most was believing that my problem was caused by rotten bosses instead of by a stubborn me. Had I not been so bullheaded, I might have realized that although I would have preferred bosses who left me alone, what I really thirsted for was respect, fulfillment, and the opportunity to do work of which I could be proud.

Had I known my true needs, I would have focused on them more clearly and I might have been better able to meet them. But I don't want to bore you with any more stories about me. How about you? What's wrong with your job? Everything? Nonsense. Saying only that you hate a job isn't enough; you have to define its faults with great specificity. Without identifying the problem, you are unlikely to solve it, and even if you get do get a new job, you may accomplish nothing other than to change your address.

TUNNEL VISION

Years ago, I worked at a company that had an annual sales meeting highlighted by a ceremony naming one of the regional managers "Salesman of the Year."* That sounds good, but becoming that company's salesman of the year was tantamount to receiving the career track kiss of death. A few of the men who claimed the award were kicked out for alleged violation of company policies, or for some equally phony excuse. Others were transferred to barren territories and later fired for being "no longer productive." Salaries froze for those who stayed, and many quit after realizing that they'd have to go elsewhere to make a decent living. The company spent a fortune hiring and training replacements, but that didn't bother Roger. He was the boss.

Saving the money spent on bonuses was not Roger's incentive in dumping the salesmen. Whatever he paid those guys may have seemed big to them and to me, but not to Roger; the man was a millionaire many times over. To understand him, you have to know that he had an insatiable ego. He

*The company had no women in sales at that point.

just *had* to be the center around which the entire company revolved. He enjoyed running the show, he liked employees to come to him for solutions to their problems, and he got a kick out of turning things around when business was slow.

Booming sales kept him from enjoying these pleasures, but Roger knew he'd look like a lunatic if he asked his sales force to stop selling. So he merely slowed them down by kicking the best performers out. Considering the state of his bank account, he felt no pain regardless of how low sales dropped.

Now don't rush to judgment and blame Roger. He made no attempt to hide his eccentricities. The company was his and he felt that he could do whatever he wanted with it. The salesmen, however, were blind to that reality. They made a big deal of being honored at each awards dinner. Charts were plastered all over the office to keep track of who was selling how much, and the buzz at the water cooler often revolved around who was going to land the biggest order in any given week or month.

This went on for years, until Michael Osborne joined the company as a regional sales manager. An extraordinarily gifted politician, Mike quickly understood what was going on. He urged Roger to scrap the awards program, arguing that it was a waste of resources that the company could better use elsewhere.

Roger agreed, and Mike broke all sales records in the following two or three years. He also made a fortune in bonuses. But he didn't go off by himself to close a big sale. He brought Roger along. Instead of hogging the kudos for everything, Mike shared the credit with Roger, who responded by sharing the wealth with Mike. And when Roger retired a few years ago, Mike became the company president.

No matter what you do, if you do it so well as to cause

resentment or insecurity in the wrong quarters, be careful. As with some of the salesmen I used to know, your heroism may get in your way.

Michael Osborne succeeded because he focused only on his top priorities—money and power. His predecessors may have had the same goals, but the awards dinner diverted their attention and visions of glory blinded them. No doubt the applause and plaques they received were of great comfort to them as they waited in line at the unemployment office.

NO PLACE FOR THE FAINT OF HEART

Job satisfaction doesn't materialize from thin air; it's the result of a significant effort. Not just any effort; hard work doesn't help unless it's the right work. No matter how many hours you expend on them, useless activities lead to useless results. Best intentions aside, however, we may not know until we've done something whether it is helps or hinders our chances of getting the satisfaction we want. Consequently, much of what we do is a risk.

Early in our careers, when we're low in the ranks, risks are relatively easy to deal with. Our obligations, power, and wealth are minimal, and so is our fear. Fifteen or twenty years later, however, everything changes. Advancement still requires taking risks, sometimes even greater risk than before. We may still lack all the satisfaction we want, but we also have mortgages, car payments, children, and other family obligations to take care of.

Given this as a backdrop, imagine yourself in a middle management job. It's not that perfect job you've always sought, but it's good enough for the moment and you think it puts you in a fine position to move up. Developments beyond your control, however, then conspire to change all that. A recession can hit, the boss you like may leave, or the company where you work may be sold to new owners with a different agenda.

Budgets are decimated and so is the payroll. You still have your job, but it's not the same. Management clearly lets you know that they expect you to put in more hours to make up for the smaller size of the workforce. They also tell you that no raises will be granted in the foreseeable future, and that if you can't work under the new regime, you will be replaced by someone else who will. In such a situation it's easy to think short term, forget long term, and put your goals on hold until your bosses say that things are better.

Don't you do it.

There are times when promotions and raises may be scarce, while new jobs are not to be found. In these circumstances, evaluate your options, go after those gains you can get, and wait for the right chance to pursue those goals that are temporarily beyond your reach. Call this a strategic retreat. It works, and although it may delay your timetable, it does so only on a short-term basis. It's the smart thing to do.

Like everyone else, you want security. So do I. But is that all you want? Of course not. Then don't sacrifice every one of your other goals just to meet the one called job security. A lot of people do this. Instead of focusing on all their goals and figuring out how to work around the obstacles in their way, they focus on their fears and foolishly see every risk as a needless risk. Every time something happens calling for them to capitalize on an opportunity, they do nothing except back down, buckle under, give up, and put their dreams on hold for fear of going too far, doing too little, acting too early, or being too late. Dictated entirely by fear, such behavior is neither strategic nor temporary. It's stupid.

You can't get security by rolling over and playing dead

every time you run up against demanding bosses or competitive, ambitious peers. No gains come without risks, and unless you are prepared to take a few bold steps once in a while, you can forget about gains.

Don't tell me you can't afford to put your job in jeopardy. If you work without job satisfaction, you will jeopardize your happiness and your self-respect. If the situation is bad enough, you may become stressed out to the point of putting your life in jeopardy. Surely your piece of mind and your health are more important than your job. But then who said anything about putting your job in jeopardy? Not I. I'll take risks, but only if they are well planned and have a good chance to succeed. Those are the only kind of risks I'll recommend to you.

The way to deal with your fears and your ego is to put your ego and security needs in perspective. Safety is an important goal, but it isn't your *only* goal. Don't let it control your thinking to the extent that your other goals can't be met.

To gain the right perspective on risks, ask yourself a few simple questions whenever you have to make a decision or take an action:

- What can I do to make certain I don't get hurt?
- What can I do if something goes wrong?
- I must have overlooked something. What is it?
- What are the weaknesses in my thinking?

To ignore your fears would be ridiculous. You can neither suppress nor forget them. I say face them head on. Figure out what they are, answer the above questions, and act accordingly. This requires neither copious notes or great preparation. All you have to do is to look before you leap and think before you act.

THINK "ME," BUT SAY "WE"

Suppose you are an advertising manager and your boss is Linda. The two of you are discussing plans for the coming year. "Unless we change our commercials," you say, "we'll will lose business." You pitch your ideas to her, and you trot out data to buttress your position, but Linda insists that your research is incomplete and your conclusions flawed. You try to argue the matter, but the more you push your viewpoint, the angrier she gets. Finally, she explodes at you and storms out of your office.

Now you're in a bind. If you give in and just let Linda have her way, you are absolutely convinced that customers will switch to your competition. You don't think Linda will fire you, but her reprisals might make you most uncomfortable if you don't give in. You can't win, can you? *Au contraire.* You most definitely *can* win, but only if you put things into perspective and refocus your thinking.

You'll never do that if all you focus on is what's good for the company. I know you're concerned about corporate welfare, and I would never suggest that you think otherwise. Your number one concern, however, should always be your own welfare.

The company is not going to let you change the advertising program. Only Linda can do that, and she may not care what's best for the company. Her priorities may be limited to considering only what is best for her. Linda may be roaring wrong—and the most shortsighted idiot you've ever met—but as long as you are under her thumb, your job is to make her happy. You can't change the advertising program unless you change Linda's mind, but you can't do that unless you motivate her to believe that *she* has nothing to lose and everything to gain.

Permit me to give you a hot news flash: It was not *your* office that Linda left in a huff. It is the property of the company and its stockholders. That desk you like so much also isn't yours, and neither are those commercials you want to change. Those things also belong to the company, and in a strange way, so does the competition that so concerns you. They aren't competing with you, but with your employer, who has brought you on as a hired hand to fight them off. If you succeed, the customers you bring in will not be yours, either. Your job, and the title on your business card belong to you, but only as long as management says they do.

You may think that an argument with Linda hinges on whether "we" will gain or lose customers, but that is simply not true. You won't lose a single customer if Linda wins the argument. Neither will Linda lose customers. Only the company will lose customers. But you've probably been brainwashed so much by your upbringing and by your bosses that you have forgotten the difference between your focus and the company's.

Bosses like us to think "we." They'll say things like "We have confidence in our new products," "We had a good year last year," "We have to work harder next time," and the old reliable "We are going to have to tighten our belts." Some managers are quite adept at using a flood of we-isms to motivate employees to focus *not* on their personal objectives, but on those imposed on them by management.

The impression you are supposed to get from a cacophony of "we" talk is that your job exists in a "one for all and all for one" environment in which employer and employee share in the rewards of success. This would be fine if it were true, but it rarely is. Totally disinterested in sharing with anyone, most corporate bosses see company goals only as vehicles with which to achieve their own personal goals.

None of this will be apparent in good times. When the

money is flowing in and they can get everything they want, even the greediest bosses may be glad to share whatever wealth remains. Once they have more power and money than they know what to do with, however, their ego drives and fears take over. They become afraid of losing what they have, and they feel constantly compelled to prove their worth. That's why they fire high achievers such as salesmen of the year.

The typical chief executive always thinks "me," meaning himself. To delude the rest of us into thinking that his intentions are honorable, he says "we." Believing him forces us into the trap of expecting that if we do a good job and help the company to be more efficient and more profitable, we will share in the wealth. Dream on. Each corporation, you see, has only so much money, and every penny you make is a penny the bosses and owners can't put in their own bank accounts.

CEOs are not the only people who may do this to you. Lower-level bosses obviously have less clout, but they all play the "we" game to differing degrees. Those of them who successfully climb the middle management ladder are masters at motivating superiors as well as subordinates.

Always say "we" to signify that you are an ally, not an adversary. Your bosses will eat it up. In contrast, saying "me"would make you look selfish and unworthy of being trusted. This may seem petty, but it isn't. In recognizing that people will be more inclined to like you if they feel that your thinking coincides with theirs, such advice bears directly on motivating others. You won't be given a raise just for making "we" talk. You will, however, make a good impression, and good impressions accumulate. Gather up enough of them over the years, and you'll command all the job satisfaction you can handle.

KEEP YOUR EGO IN CHECK

You are a veritable genius. I know that and so does your ego. We're both impressed, but unlike your ego, I'm willing to presume that your career plan, if you have one, needs shoring up in certain areas. If that plan seems perfect, don't believe it. Search for weaknesses and correct them. Your ego gets you into trouble when it fools you into thinking that you are always right, that you can't lose, and that yours are the only needs and opinions that matter.

One of the fastest ways to lose focus is to engage in the screwed-up thinking that is inevitable whenever people give in to their egos. Let's return to the story I told earlier about a boss named Linda getting mad after the two of you argued over advertising plans. What would your focus be in such a situation? To prove that you are right and that she is wrong? To be recognized as the repository of all truth and wisdom? Nah. You're not petty enough for shallow think ing like that. Neither are you stupid enough to get angry and confront an adversary when the both of you are agitated.

Be sensitive to simple disagreements that turn into heated arguments. Don't let them get that far. Maintain your focus, gather your thoughts, lay low, keep calm, and don't let things get out of control. Back off and say nothing more about the matter until you are better prepared to motivate the other person, and when he or she might be more receptive to agreeing with you.

Unfortunately, a powerful adversary will be fighting you every step of the way: not your boss—your ego. Unable and unwilling to wait, egos demand instant gratification, not promises of delayed satisfaction. Paying little or no attention to the consequences you may have to face tomorrow, that ego of yours will do whatever it can to make you take action that will let you feel good today.

Your ego may be enraged at the thought of having to walk on eggshells when you argue with someone who is blatantly wrong. It will tug at you without letup to intellectually grind your adversary into the ground. Or, it might force you to concentrate on how smart you are and how stupid the other person is. That's focus, but it's the head-in-the-sand type, not the gaze-at-the-sky type.

You may find this difficult to believe in the case of some individuals, but each of us thinks, some more clearly than others. We do not think in lockstep, however. No matter how brilliant you are, people will occasionally disagree with you. The best way to deal with differences of opinion is to get them out in the open and discuss them calmly, with both sides focusing on finding a resolution. This is impossible if you surrender to the demands of your ego and focus on feeling insulted or threatened.

Do whatever you can to prevent your ego from dragging you into an argument in which the participants feel that their honor or security is at stake. No matter who started the fray, the moment one of you begins lobbing verbal grenades, the other person will fight back. Soon the battle will escalate, and you will be up to your eyeballs focusing on the argument rather than on the quest for job satisfaction.

By engaging in office warfare, you risk focusing only on humiliating or defeating your enemies. The angrier you get at people, the more you will focus on hurting them instead of on helping yourself. Focus on revenge if you like, but don't complain to me if your raises or promotions later on are unsatisfactory or nonexistent.

If you can't resist the pull of your ego, give in to it. Address the people who offended you or got in your way, and tell them off in the bluntest, vilest language you can imagine. Vent your spleen at full throttle and don't stop until you have covered everything that bothers you, and that includes past indiscretions you haven't complained about in several months or years.

Just be certain you do none of this in person, and not even over the telephone. Write it all out in a letter, making sure you have said everything you want to say. Don't mail that letter; keep it in your desk drawer for a day or so. When you get back to it, give it a once-over for accuracy, grammar, and spelling. Put it away again, this time for at least two days. Then read it carefully. Does the writer of that letter come across as an adult or as an immature crybaby? Be honest with yourself, and I'll bet you decide against sending that letter anywhere except to the circular file beneath your desk.

Writing a letter in these situations has four advantages:

- It gives your ego that temporary gratification it craves.
- It brings you back to reality by showing you how silly you can be.
- It may calm you down enough to remember that your focus is *not* on gaining points in a put-down contest.
- While writing or checking the letter, you will be seated at your desk, obviously hard at work, and probably with an intense look on your face. This is just the kind of image your boss will want to see. If you don't tell him what you're really doing, I won't.

PRIORITIES

Focus is rarely a clear-cut concentration on a single goal. Each of us has many goals that will occasionally be in conflict, putting us in the position of having to set priorities and to choose one over another.

Here's an example of how focus fits in with priorities. Put yourself in the shoes of an engineering manager. Assume for now that the size is right, and don't worry if you know nothing about engineering (many engineering managers are in the same boat). Your boss tells you to accept several drastic budget cuts and also to pressure your top designer—who has been with the company for thirty years—into taking early retirement. Although this designer knows the company's products better than anyone else, he also makes more money than a lot of other people. Management wants to replace him with someone right out of graduate school. The new guy would have no experience, but he'd work cheap.

"These budget reductions are suicidal," you say to yourself. "We'll never be able to get anything done." You tell your boss, however, that you'll do everything you can, but that your job will be hard to perform at the lower funding. Is he swayed? No. He doesn't care how difficult *your* job will be. He's sweating over only one job—his own. His goal is to look like a hero to *his* bosses for ruthlessly cutting costs.

You also don't want to lose your best performer. He's a friend of yours, and you're personally offended at having to put him out to pasture. But the boss says: "This isn't age discrimination, it's fiscal responsibility." What would you do in a case like this? When it happened to me, I raised a mighty noise, refusing in advance to accept any responsibility for the consequences. On more than one occasion, I was able to save someone from the ax.

You've been down the same road, but this time, the boss explains his logic more bluntly by saying that if you won't do what he wants, "I'll get rid of you *and* your old-man designer." This brutal approach clearly puts your goals into conflict with his. What the boss wants to do is shortsighted and foolish. But those negatives are valid only if we focus on the long-range good of the company. Is that the boss's focus? Obviously not.

As much as you want to do a good job and keep your friend from losing his, you certainly don't want to lose yours. Be careful as you ponder your choices. "We" may not be terribly efficient in "our" design work after making the cuts the boss wants made, but *you* will still have your job.

Who would you put first—you, your friend, or the boss? I can't tell you how to answer that question. That's up to you. All I can say is that unless you're careful, your status can change in a second from that of an inner circle "we" to one of "them" who was sacked for not paying enough attention to the boss's priorities.

3

Take Action

Jim Taylor was the customer service manager at Armark Industries in Perth Amboy. After twelve years with the company, Jim could stand his job no longer. He didn't dislike the work; it was his boss that bugged him. The two of them never agreed on the role and importance of customer service. Rightly or wrongly, Jim felt shackled and unappreciated. Worst of all, he couldn't stand his boss's reluctance to take advice, his refusal to thank anyone, or his insistence on unquestioned obedience. The way to succeed with that boss was to tell him only what he wanted to hear. Jim complied, but he wanted out.

Jim did *not*, however, grumble about his income. He was well paid, perhaps *too* well paid for his own good. As far as he could tell, his take-home was nearly 40 percent more than what other companies were paying for the same work. He was so enthralled with the money that, for a long time, he put up with working conditions he never should have tolerated. By the time he admitted his misery to himself, Jim had missed out on many opportunities he might have gotten had he pursued them when he was younger and more attractive to other employers.

After sending an attractive résumé to hundreds of companies, Jim got a few offers, but only a couple of them were willing to pay enough. Unfortunately, they were out of town, in places Jim had never heard of. He had spent his whole life within an hour's drive of New York. Moving to the sticks was an unacceptable solution to him, and he wasn't about to impose such a move on his family.

Poor Jim. He didn't live lavishly, but he and his wife had bills to pay. Nothing out of the ordinary; just the usual house, tax, car, clothing, food, and utility expenses. In addition, they had a son in college. That alone cost more than twenty thousand dollars a year. Who has that kind of spare cash lying around? Do you? I don't, and neither did the Taylors. They wound up mortgaging themselves to the gills. No way could Jim afford to take a job paying appreciably less money than he was making at Armark.

"I have no choice," Jim used to say. He was convinced that he had to stay where he was, to keep that job he hated, and to continue tolerating his boss's behavior. Jim is a bright guy, but he was wrong. Scads of choices were at his disposal. He just never knew they existed.

MULTIPLE CHOICES

The only way to get job satisfaction from a terrible job is to *create change*. No, I'm not talking about nickels and dimes. Nor do I mean that job satisfaction would be yours merely by waiting for your boss to change. *You* have to change your attitude, your tactics for getting along with him, or both. In the absence of divine intervention, he will stick to his Neanderthal ways unless you motivate him do otherwise. If you want to change his mind on a matter the two you have already discussed, change your argument or your way of presenting it. Unless you give him an incentive to change, he won't.

You can take seven types of action to increase job satisfaction:

1. **Change conditions on your current job.** The following chapters discuss how to do this.
2. **Change your source of satisfaction.** Does your job have to provide all your joys? I sure hope not.
3. **Change jobs** if you can.
4. **Change your profession.** If you don't like your line of work, try another.
5. **Change your lifestyle.** Lower your expenses and you may be able to afford a better job that pays less.
6. **Change your address.** A different neighborhood may mean a more affordable mortgage or rent payments. A different city may put you closer to better jobs.
7. **Moan, groan, feel sorry for yourself, and blame everyone else for all your problems.** You're not stupid enough to do only this, are you?

The beauty of these options is that you can use as many or as few as you like. Indeed, you should try all of them except the last. I know it's popular, easy, and feels good, but it accomplishes nothing except to prolong your pain, so don't waste your time with it.

There may not be any decent jobs out there for you right now, you may not want to change professions, your lifestyle may already be pared to the bone, and moving right now might place great hardship on your family. You may think this puts you in an impossible situation, but it doesn't. Jim Taylor thought he was in an impossible situation. He felt trapped in a job he hated but from which he felt he could not escape.

He was wrong, and so are you if you feel you're stuck without options because you can't find a different job. As long as some judge didn't assign you to the one you have, it's not a jail. You can still influence the conditions under which you work, and you can change your sources of satisfaction. It is no coincidence that these are the first two options on the list and the focus of this book.

You may have irrevocably decided to leave, but months or perhaps years may pass before you find the right job. Use changes to make life as livable as possible in the interim, make the best of the job you still have, and always try to fix it before you give up on it.

Keep your focus and never lose sight of what you're trying to fix. Fix only those things that, if repaired, will benefit you directly. If fixing something won't result in a gain to you, don't churn up your guts worrying about it. Forget it. Spend your time only on matters that can help you reach your goals. Let the company's CEO worry about the other stuff. It's about time he started to earn all those big bucks he gets.

PLANS

Others might tell you to focus on realistic career goals, but not me. I hate to see people give up on their dreams because some "expert" has pronounced those dreams unrealistic. Many goals are incredibly hard to reach, but that doesn't mean they are unrealistic; it means only that you need an incredibly good plan to reach them. Many people have attained seemingly unreachable goals by singlemindedness, force of will, and a good plan.

Even though you know your boss has been increasing salaries by only three or four percent, for example, you might decide to fight for a 10 percent raise. This is okay if you would be satisfied with 10 percent, and if that's the case, stick with your decision. For that matter, if you'd be happy with 4 percent, take it. My interest is in helping you to get what you do want, not to presume to know better than you what you *should* want. However, neither 3 nor 10 percent might be acceptable to you. Your needs and your dreams may lead you to want to double your income in the next year. That's okay too; doubling is what you want, so that's what you should gear up to get. This does not mean that you should devise an argument for convincing your boss to give you a 100 percent raise. With all but a very few bosses, that *would* be unrealistic.

Suppose, however, that you can get a 10 percent raise, and maybe another 30 percent from a second job. That's 40 percent. Can you think of anything else you might do? How about a part-time business on weekends? Maybe that can make up the difference. If not, perhaps you can sell something or borrow the rest. Difficult? Yes. Risky? It could be, if you stretch yourself too thin. It's also short range; you can borrow or sell for only so long before getting in more trouble than you'd ever want. But is the scheme realistic? Given the right details and a lot of hard work, you bet it is!

Unless you choose off-the-wall, impossible goals, they probably *are* realistic. The means you use for meeting them may be unrealistic. Those means have a name—plans. You can make good career changes only with a good plan.

To increase your chances of getting a new job, you may have to send your résumé to hundreds of companies. If you set aside two hours a night Monday through Friday and six hours every weekend, you figure you could type out the envelopes, résumés, and cover letters to a hundred companies over a seven-day span. That's just about fifteen a day. In the space of a month, you could get more than four hundred résumés in the mail. Guess what? That's a plan. It's not elaborate, but it is a plan.

The only problem with your plan is that before you send résumés to four hundred companies, you have to decide what to say in those résumés. You may have to spend a few days drafting your words, so give yourself a week for that task. But don't think you're finished. You can't mail résumés to four hundred companies unless you first determine which companies those are. You certainly don't want to send out envelopes addressed only to "To whom it may concern." Spend some time identifying the right recipients. That's going to take another week, but it's a necessary week, so include it in your plan.

Whatever their shapes or lengths, all plans include four elements:

- What you want
- When you want it
- How you expect to get it or reach it in that time frame
- A way to tell whether you are proceeding satisfactorily

As long as you have a plan, you can rate your progress as you go along, and you can make changes before you go too far in the wrong direction. Without a plan, you're lucky to go anyplace but in circles.

WHAT IF?

You may not know it, but you probably do have a career plan. Everybody has a career plan of sorts. The only objective many people have is to support themselves and their families. Their timetable? The rest of their lives. Their plan is simple. By working hard, doing good work, and earning all the raises they can get, they hope to pay their bills. There is nothing wrong with such a plan, but if that's where it stops, it may not be enough for you.

All career plans are based on assumptions. We assume that

- the high hopes we have at the start of a job will be realized,
- the economy will be stable,
- the companies where we work will be well managed,
- technology or other factors will not make our jobs obsolete,
- the good times we enjoy will continue unabated, and
- our bosses will be reasonable and fair.

These assumptions may or may not come true, but the biggest problem with most of them is that they concern matters that are beyond our control. You cannot prevent the economy from going haywire, and you probably have no control over management's wisdom or lack thereof. What you *can* control is the course of your career plan if your assumptions prove wrong at any point in time.

Many people blame management stupidity or greed for their job difficulties. They may also blame the economy, but a more likely culprit is a lack of contingency planning. You will never be able take charge of your career until you get into the habit of developing a "What if . . . ?" plan that you

can instantly adopt if your original plan fails to function satisfactorily. Such contingency thinking is commonly known
as a "Plan B." You can always decline to develop contingency plans, but if that's what you do, you will suffer for
your shortsightedness. To set up a Plan B, ask and answer a
bunch of "What would I do if. . . . ?" questions about how
you would expect to recover in the event that things do not
go your way.

When a friend of mine lost his job and his unemployment
compensation expired, he used to awaken at 4 A.M. every day
to deliver newspapers for a couple of hours, and then go to
work again selling computer products. However, those jobs
didn't pay enough, so he taught word processing at the local
community college three nights a week. I don't know where
he found the strength, but his plans worked for several
months until he found a new job. What he did might not
work for you, but that's no problem. Pick your own Plan B.

MILESTONES

Getting job satisfaction requires you to motivate your boss all
year long, but you don't have to wait until the end of the year
to see if your plan is working. A good plan includes milestones that allow you to gauge your progress and make mid-
course corrections as necessary.

Is the boss reacting positively? Once you get to know him,
look for signs that can tell you whether you are succeeding. If
he has nice things to say, you know you are going in the right
direction. If he says nothing, ask him how you did after you
have completed a task. Did he get what he expected? Was it
on time? Could you have done more? Should you have done
anything differently? The biggest companies in the world

check their business strategies by frequently asking their customers such questions. As long as you do not make a pest of yourself, there is no reason why you could not do the same with your boss.

Set a milestone one, two, or three months away. See how you are doing. If the boss is reacting positively, continue as planned. But if he seems turned off by what you have been doing, try Plan B. If that doesn't work, go to Plan C, and then to Plan D, and even to Plan E, if you must.

Plan evaluation will be easier if your objectives are measurable. "More money" is not a useful goal. Think in terms of a "10 percent raise," on the other hand, and you can easily determine whether you are on schedule for reaching it. Not everything can be quantified, but any time you can assign a "how many," "how much," or "when" to an objective, do so. If you don't succeed, and you have no Plan B, or if you have one and elect to do nothing anyway, don't complain to me.

ALTERNATIVE SOURCES

Some years ago I worked for John Burke, a man who had to have the last word on everything. He just couldn't bear to give me the slightest latitude to act on my own. I was supposed to be his advertising manager, but every time I wrote something, he found something wrong with it. Whether it was an ad, a press release, the company newsletter, or a product data sheet, he rewrote it, and then he'd criticize me for the mistakes he claimed I made when I wrote it. John seemed to draw great satisfaction from making a spectacle of loudly criticizing me during staff meetings.

John loved to tell people that I was not perfect. He was

right. I think I'm a pretty good writer, but I cannot proof-read my own work. I just won't see many of my own mistakes, so I am not entirely surprised when someone tries to help by pointing where I have goofed. John Burke's objective, however, was not to make corrections; most of the changes he demanded were trivial and matters of personal style. His main goal was to put me in my place as a person who allegedly couldn't be trusted and consequently had to knuckle under to his greater wisdom.

Working for John upset me a great deal when I started with him, but after a while I found a way to greatly diminish the impact of his nonsense. At the same time that he was telling everyone in his company what a lousy writer I was, I had become the author of two books. One of those books was on writing, and I also taught writing at several colleges. The world apparently thought I was a decent writer. John didn't think so, but his focus was on being the boss, which does not necessarily produce the same results that would stem from a focus on getting the best writing.

When I couldn't get the fulfillment I needed at work, I did my creating at night. I learned not take John's criticism personally. Of course his carping bothered me, but I could live with it; I had alternate sources of satisfaction.

You don't need to be a writer to have your own alternatives, you need goals, plans, and resourcefulness in your use of time. Some people find their alternatives in a part-time business. That's what writing became to me. I know a woman who is a first-grade teacher. She never really hated her job, but after a number of years, she tired of dealing so exclusively with young children. After normal working hours, she became the sales representative for an educational software company. What a match. She augmented her income considerably, but money wasn't her goal. Her goal was to spend more time working with adults and that's what she did.

Surely you can do something after hours to get at least some of the satisfaction you can't get on the job. With some people, this means a second job, getting involved in local politics, taking on a hobby, or volunteering their time for a worthy cause. What might the right alternatives be for you?

COMMITMENT

In case you are wondering, I didn't forget to tell you the end of the Jim Taylor story. He's the guy who allowed an oversized salary to hold him in a nothing job. Sad to say, Jim fell into a rut. As soon as he decided that he hated his job, he lost his enthusiasm for it. He didn't care anymore. He went through the motions, and he was able to satisfy the boss who hired him, but eventually a new boss came in and Jim just couldn't change accordingly.

Jim had spent too many years doing what his old boss told him to do, while totally neglecting important activities such as establishing a good reputation and keeping up to date on the latest techniques in his field. By the time the new boss came on board and started modernizing, Jim was too deeply rooted in old habits. A shadow of the person he had been when he started, he couldn't keep up, and he was eventually fired.

Jim was forced to take a different kind of job in a different city. The move was difficult, but neither Jim nor anyone in his family melted or turned to stone when they took up residence in an unfamiliar neighborhood in a faraway state. It wasn't easy, but they survived. They had no decent alternative. The Taylors wanted none of the changes that were forced upon them, but none of them wanted to live in a cardboard box or to starve. That was their reality, and once they recognized it, the changes they had to make were easy.

Most of us never get cranked up about our careers unless we are forced to do so. We say we hate our jobs, but until disaster strikes, we're always too busy to do anything about making the changes we want. Consequently, we wind up having to live with all the less desirable changes that life heaps on us.

To avoid that, make a commitment now never ever to accept a lack of job satisfaction. If a job isn't what you want it to be and you can't find other employment right away, don't just sit there and tolerate it. Do something now to change it. If that doesn't produce a result you can live with, do something else.

The only change you must *not* make is to slow down and slack off where you are now. That would be not only sophomoric, but also a sure way to upset bosses. As bad as yours is now, he can get worse, and you have to be careful not to force his hand in that direction. Once he feels that you no longer care about his interests, he sure as hell won't care about yours.

·············4············

I Scratch Your Back, You Scratch Mine

You have no value to the company where you work. None. For that matter, you have no value to *any* company. But don't take that personally. Nobody has value to a company. This is because companies are nothing more than legal entities— papers of incorporation, tax returns, and other things. Companies can't think on their own. Neither can they give you a raise, a promotion, or a better job. They have no needs, and they are incapable of making value judgments. Those can be made only by people. If you want to be happier on the job, stop trying to make yourself valuable to a company. Make yourself valuable to the people who run that company. How do you do that? By helping them meet their needs.

What are those needs—to see that the company does well? No. People need to make certain that *they* do well. Since their success does not necessarily make anyone else happy, how- ever, the job they want you to do may not coincide with the job you'd like to do. If you wind up chasing goals that are different from those of your boss, the two of you will continuously be at odds. Even if your ideas are better than his, he's the boss and you're not, so he decides whose ideas are used, and you can be certain they won't be yours.

Monty Clark taught me this lesson many years ago. Monty was the president of a company that made television parts, and he hired me to manage his plant in Cincinnati. I put the regional salespeople on a bonus plan that rewarded them handsomely if they reached certain goals. Sales doubled as a result, the sales force made big bucks, and everybody was happy. Everybody but Monty, that is. Monty never liked the bonus plan. When I brought it up, he disputed my claim that the plan would increase sales. But I fought for my position, I pestered him for approval, and he finally gave in to me.

My predictions proved true from day one. Business just rolled in, but Monty was annoyed that a couple of our salespeople made more money than he did. Every few months he'd ask me to scrap the plan, even though sales were still climbing. As president, he felt that his income should be more than anyone else in the company. Whenever he suggested we change back to our old ways, however, I asked him whether he wanted to revert back to the old level of sales.

The fourth year of my stewardship in Cincinnati saw the emergence of inflation, followed by a recession. Sales dipped sharply. This upset me because I was judged on performance, and any loss of business would certainly reduce my income. My regional managers were also upset.

Monty seemed almost gleeful despite the downturn. Totally ignoring the facts and the recession, he forced me to revise our entire compensation program and restrict big bonuses. My better salespeople soon left for greener pastures.

I respected Monty Clark, and for years I thought that he had lost his mind, walking away from millions of dollars of profitable sales just to avoid paying big bonuses to a few people. But all that is now history. We tried to hire a new batch of regional managers, but Monty refused to offer enough to attract top talent. Sales never again approached anything near the peak levels in the good years. Monty blamed me for that. And then he fired me.

His motives made no sense until I realized that his actions had nothing to do with sales, profits, or anything else related to how well the company was doing. Monty didn't do what he did because he cared about the company. Of course he wanted the business to survive and be solvent enough to afford him, but he was already making good money when I arrived. Monty didn't need more money, he needed only to be right. I proved him wrong on the bonus plan and he never forgave me for that.

My mistake was being the person who kept him from fulfilling his need. You could say that I didn't care enough about Monty, but the truth is that I didn't care at all about him. I cared only about "the company," but it had no way of returning the favor and caring about me. Had I paid more attention to Monty and less attention to sales, the company might have lost out, but I would have gained considerably.

POLITICS

Why would people do anything for you? Because they think you are competent, nice, or well-intentioned? Not likely. People will do things that benefit you if they believe that you will do (or have already done) things that benefit them.

There's a word for this—politics. The power behind that word is the engine that transforms a bunch of disorganized individuals into a workforce that functions harmoniously. Politics does not have to be underhanded or sleazy. It can be right out in the open and everybody can share in its rewards as long as they follow a simple theme: "I scratch your back, you scratch mine."

This may be revolting at first thought. You may not like being in the same room with some people, much less touching them. The thought of their touching you may be even more disgusting, but don't even think of that. Now don't misinterpret me. As you are about to discover, scratching backs is by no stretch of the imagination the same as kissing backsides. "Back-scratching" is merely a figure of speech to remind you that politics is *trading*. In return for what you need, you must be willing and able to give another person what he or she needs.

This is the path taken by elected officials. These are the wonderful folks you have voted into power in town hall, the statehouse, Congress, and the White House. A few of them are good at what they do, but most of them are good only at making speeches and looking great on television. They have one characteristic in common: their main concern is with keeping their jobs, and their main talent is for getting elected and reelected. They are experts at making promises they can't meet, and geniuses at blaming their failure to deliver on people or events beyond their control.

Politics in the workplace is different, but not all *that* different. Office politicians promise far more than they ever deliver. They know all about being promoted, maximizing their job security, getting raises, and making certain they garner other forms of favoritism for themselves. Most of them will do nothing for you unless you have done (or probably will do) something for them.

You may think that a particular individual is the lowest of the low, perhaps the most loathsome citizen in the galaxy. Yet if you urgently need something for which he is the only source, you may gladly give him whatever he wants in return for it. This is what Charles Dudley Warner must have meant when he said: "Politics makes strange bedfellows." You don't have to climb into the sack with those whose favors you need, but you must nonetheless find ways to scratch their backs.

You will like some of the people with whom you have to work, while finding others to be nothing short of despicable. Unless your purpose in working is to make friends, however, forget consideration of whom you like or don't like, and concentrate solely on whom you *need*.

PERCEPTIONS

Sucking up to an obnoxious boss is probably not your idea of what should be going on in a workers' paradise. It isn't mine either. Being a doormat is repugnant. But who says you have to be a doormat? I don't. Neither do many dictatorial bosses. They don't want you to be a doormat. That is merely our *perception* of what they want.

We can never achieve satisfaction unless we learn to recognize what is true in our lives and what is false. The ability to distinguish between those extremes is a function of how clearly we see things, how objectively we see ourselves, and how logically we interpret what we see. Our thinking, however, is never entirely logical. It is clouded by instincts and emotions, so we have difficulty seeing the whole truth in an absolute sense. The best we can do in peering through those clouds is to see our *perception* of the truth.

Politics is based on the premise that what counts in determining human behavior is the way we react to our perception of the truth, not the truth itself. In the motivational arena, perceptions are everything and facts mean nothing. This does not mean you should lie. You don't have to lie to be good at politics. What you have to do is to carefully select which truths you volunteer and which ones you emphasize when making a point.

To motivate with perceptions, you must make people believe that:

- You can be helpful to them in meeting their needs.
- You have their interests in mind.
- Your thinking aligns with theirs or does not conflict with theirs.
- You are not a threat to their power or their ability to do what they want to do.
- You are loyal only to them.

Other than hero-worshipers, fanatics, or fools, who would meet all these qualifications? Viewed with the icy stare of logic, no one. Unless you are engaged in a religious or social cause, you would never put someone else's needs before your own.

You can, however, make people *perceive* that you put their interests before yours. This is the Achilles' heel of egocentric people. Completely focused on *their* needs and *their* problems, they forget that the rest of us have our own interests. Putting them first seems so natural to them that they will not question your motives when you do it. Instead, they will sense a liking for you.

IMAGE IS EVERYTHING

The more certain you are of yourself, the more assertive you will be, the less likely you will be to take no for an answer, and the more effective you will be at convincing others to go along with you.

But suppose you are not all that confident of your position. Someone who is meek, wishy-washy, and unsure of himself can rarely persuade anyone to do anything. What if you have reservations? Can you motivate someone else to do something if you don't believe in it yourself? Good salespeople do that all the time by suppressing their own views and focusing on meeting customer needs.

In the event that this is not your style, you can always fall back on what has always struck me as one of the most basic flaws in human thinking. When we encounter a person who is smartly dressed, impeccably groomed, and well-spoken, we automatically perceive him or her to have all the best in human qualities: competence, intelligence, reliability, loyalty, and possibly even a gross dislike of daytime talk shows.

No matter what you really are, if you dress well enough, stand tall, speak assertively, and sport the latest hairstyle, you will be perceived as indistinguishable from the nicest, most law-abiding people on earth. New colleagues will form a first impression that you should be accepted and even trusted.

Acceptance is a matter of looking and acting like those in power. This has always been a problem for minorities who dress, speak, and look different from the majority. If you still think that competence and productivity are all that count in business, consider that for centuries, untold thousands of exceptionally qualified individuals have been rejected for jobs and promotions just because of their skin color or their ethnic background. Most educated people in our society are not that ignorant these days, but they *are* stupid enough to be impressed by factors as hollow and meaningless as whether your clothes are smartly color-coordinated.

Scoff at the value of appearance if you like, but I strongly urge that you instead take advantage of it and develop a reputation characterized by the Sunday smile, the pressed suit, the genial handshake, and the businesslike tone of voice. These things may add nothing to productivity or profits, but that's merely a fact, and facts don't mean beans when they're thrown up against the power of perceptions and images!

Once you achieve the right image sartorially, turn things up a notch by looking at people right between their eyes when you talk to them. You will look far more confident than you would if you glanced off to the side or down at the ground. You don't have to be belligerent or aggressive, but if you come across as positive that you are right in a dispute, your adversary may blink and back down before you do.

FOLLOW YOUR LEADER

You might ask why you have to deal in perceptions and images while so many powerful people never play politics. Why not do what many of them do and terrorize everyone? The answers are simple; they *do* play politics and they do *not* terrorize everyone. Terror is the tool they use to keep some of us in line, but you had better believe that fear is the last feeling they work to engender in the hearts of *their* bosses, customers, or others over whom they have no direct control.

Consider also the gutless wonder who follows rules and regulations to the extreme of hiding behind them rather than taking bold actions. You may think he is a loser, but he succeeds because he convinces his bosses that his unwillingness to take risks provides them with security.

Another example is the person I call the albatross. Virtually useless from the standpoint of productivity, he not only stays on the job, he gets promoted. Why? Because his bosses perceive him as being so inept that he is no threat to them.

The biggest politician of all is the con artist. Smoother

than greased lightning, this character promises everything, delivers selectively, charms your socks off if he wants more from you, and stabs you in the back if he sees you as an enemy. No matter what you think of him, learn from his example. He may have disappointed you once or twice, but that never happens to the people he needs most consistently. He always makes sure that they are always happy, even if no one else is.

You may be none of these people, or you may be all of them, each on different occasions or under different circumstances. Or, you may fit only a mold of your own. What works for someone else, however, might not fit with your unique combination of personality and talents. Your best bet will be to pick and choose ideas from the behavior of others, but to cultivate a political style of your own.

POLITICAL DOS AND DONT'S

Do:

- be careful. There can be a fine line between someone's scratching your back and thrusting a political knife into it.
- try to get into the habit of looking at people not as bosses, managers, researchers, engineers, accountants, lawyers, plumbers, etc., but as individual human beings who will be responsive to your needs if you are responsive to theirs.
- say things like *please, may I, thank you,* and *you're welcome.* You should try to put people at ease, not to make them tense and suspicious of you. Gas pains may be the cause of your brusque demeanor and that tortured look on your face, but the people you are trying to motivate may assume that you are angry, distrustful, and aggressive.

- act interested and listen to people, no matter how pointless their conversations may be. This isn't hard; all you have to do is pay attention, nod approvingly, and say things like "That's interesting" or "Really?" at appropriate intervals.
- treat everybody's needs as important. Those at the bottom of the ladder may not be able to do much for you now, but you never know who may be in a position to be a big help later.
- always be on the lookout for ways in which you can praise people for their ideas, their appearance, or anything else of which they may be proud.
- go out of your way to befriend and meet the needs of the people on whom the bosses in your life depend. Bosses spend a lot of time out of your reach traveling and sitting in meetings, but their secretaries and assistants are usually easy to find. They may not divulge confidential information, but they could be helpful to you if you are nice to them.
- cultivate a reputation for trustworthiness.
- pay attention to little things. If people don't feel they can rely on you for small matters, they certainly won't depend on you for the big stuff.
- pay homage to your boss if you do anything to hype yourself. Possibilities here include using reports as a platform for his approval signature, or to share credit with him and thank him for his contributions.
- look at politics not as a chance to scam people or to hurt them, but as an opportunity to exchange favors of real value.
- remember that perceptions are infinitely more powerful than facts.

Don't:

- wait for people to scratch your back before you scratch theirs. Act first. Even if someone has never done anything nice for you, do something nice for her. Your objective in taking this route is twofold: to get others to depend upon you for meeting their needs, and to put them in your debt.
- sulk or give up if someone fails to immediately shower you with gratitude after you "scratch his back." You may have to scratch for some time before the itch goes away.
- grovel at anyone's feet begging for opportunities to meet his or her needs. Such behavior is offensive and will cause others to perceive you as a loser.
- be obvious when meeting needs. Speak matter-of-factly, don't make a scene, don't wink or smile, and don't gloat.
- make promises you know you can't keep. Go out on a limb to any extent you are comfortable, but use politics to build a reputation as someone who delivers, not as someone who lies.
- fail to keep promises without making amends, updating the original promise, or, at the very least, attributing your failure to a scapegoat whose complicity will absolve you of any blame.
- focus only on what you think is important. You may in fact be correct, but that won't matter if everyone else believes that you are wrong.
- go over your boss's head or behind his back to make him look bad or to make yourself look good at his expense. He may look at such behavior as evidence of disloyalty, and deal with you most unpleasantly. Beyond that, his bosses may frown on you for bothering them with your problems.

- make enemies. Down the road, they generally will not be as nice (or as useful) to you as friends.
- forget that *people*—not companies—have needs.

Most important, don't underestimate people, and don't think that they are stupid just because their priorities, methods, or opinions are not the same as yours. The person to whom you report may think that denial is a strictly Egyptian phenomenon, but if you think that makes him easy prey for shrewd manipulations, you may be the one who is hiding from reality. If you must make an assumption about someone, err on the safe side and presume that he is at least as smart as you are, if not more so. When you look down on someone, he or she may sense it, dislike you, and decide to retaliate.

Similarly, don't just act "as if" you are interested in whether people meet their needs. You may not give a damn as to whether they are happy, but if you want them to help meet your needs, you'd better make sure you really do get worked up about theirs. If all you can do is put on an act, they'll probably see right through you.

A MEANS TO AN END

As I have described it, politics is a type of horse trading in which you give up something of value with the intention of getting something back of equal or greater value. Trade your hard work, your expertise, and your courage for job satisfaction, but do not trade your self-respect. That can easily happen if you allow your career to be controlled by bosses who demand everything and refuse to give anything in return.

Some sickos and emotional misfits get their jollies by being feared or otherwise taking unfair advantage of people. Not satisfied with supervising you, they want to control you to the point where they destroy your will to resist them. You can't keep them at bay using only the politics I've described in this chapter, but with a little guts and the right smarts, you *can* handle them better than you can by doing nothing but a good job. I'll show you how in chapters 7, 13, and 14.

You may say that being political is obnoxious, if not degrading, that all this is risky, and that creating the kinds of perceptions I've suggested is not your style. You may be right, but so what? That's head-in-the-sand thinking. I'm not suggesting that you cheat, attack, or kill anyone. You don't even have to maim. I recommend merely taking a sensible initiative instead of taking it on the chin when people try to take advantage of you.

You've already tried the work-hard-and-worry-about-the-company routine, and you've discovered that it doesn't get you very far. Congratulations on finally waking up. Politics is the best way for you to get what you deserve. Master it and you will be able to engage in some horse trading of your own design to get more job satisfaction. As I hope you will soon find out firsthand, there's nothing at all degrading about that.

............5............

Observe and Test

The biggest challenge involved in meeting someone's needs is to figure out what those needs are. People do not wear signs that say "oppressive pig," "coward," "liar," "scum of the earth," or anything else that would give you clues about how to deal with them. Neither do they register for their needs at Bloomingdale's.

Figuring out other people's needs is far from easy. You can always ask bosses and colleagues what they want from you, but the answers you get will in all probability be sanitized for your consumption and related to their work, not to their deepest needs. People often have a hidden agenda. Suppose, for example, your boss tells you to put off making what you think is an important business trip. He says he is worried about falling profits and that he wants to cut expenses, but his strongest motivation may be that he's afraid of hurting his reputation or losing his job.

If the purpose of the trip is to book a large order, for example, he might rather lose the order than close it and let you get the credit. Had you asked him to come along in the first place, he might not be so upset about your going. If you think this is ridiculous, or downright childish, you're right. If you think it isn't prevalent, however, you're quite wrong.

What does your boss *really* want? He may want to confirm that his thinking is governed by the brilliance of his logic. Logic indeed often does influence how we get things done, but wants and needs are typically controlled by six factors that have nothing to do with logic: jealousy, greed, anger, pride, ego, and fear. He may not know this, in which case he won't know what he wants.

Even if he does understand his motivations, however, your leader may not tell you about his weaknesses. You can't expect him to take you into his confidence and admit that he is terrified of being laid off or that he is driven by a level of selfishness unmatched in the history of western civilization.

Your boss asks you to design a product, revamp a system, sell to a customer, or reword a press release. He represents his intentions to be honorable, and he claims profits, productivity, or sales will go up if you do what he asks. He tells you everyone in the company will benefit. You are happy to comply, but is that *all* he wants? Unless he is a recent candidate for sainthood, he wants to reap personal benefit from your work. Will he be upset if you benefit and he doesn't? I don't know, but to be on the safe side, assume that he would like to benefit at least as much as you.

You are asking for trouble if you try to motivate him by randomly guessing at his needs or by assuming that he has the same needs as anyone else. Not all bosses, for example, are dictators. Yours might even appreciate someone who plays devil's advocate in a constructive way. Beneath all their bravado, bosses are in many ways the same as the rest of us: trying to survive, afraid of screwing up, and occasionally in need of someone with whom to share ideas and concerns without feeling uncomfortable.

All humans have similar needs, but we don't reveal those needs in the same way or to the same degree. Every one of us is unique in terms of what we like or hate. So sharpen your focus on that one person you want to motivate. Identify *his* needs, not yours, and not those of the boss you had last year. As much as you might want to bring all your current and past bosses together at the bottom of the sea, you can't lump them together when it comes to motivational strategies.

One of the biggest mistakes you can make in assessing needs is to ask what would make sense for a given individual to do in a given situation. Forget about making sense. The question is not what you think someone *should* do, but rather what he or she *will* do.

And that's not the only question. What turns him on or off? What makes him feel better or worse when he is under pressure? What makes him feel safe? Who are his favorite associates? Which ones are most successful at getting what they want from him? Maybe he would treat you better if you related to him the way they do.

CHECK IT OUT

Don't just look at what people are doing. Figure out why they are doing it. Someone's words may be giving you one message, but you should look at body language, facial expressions, and tone of voice to seek out the meaning behind those words.

Rub your eyes, blow the wax out of your ears, and focus your attention on observing others to figure out their needs. The more you do this, the more you'll learn about motivating. You should ideally watch a person for several months before committing yourself to a particular course of action, but that is not always possible, so give it as much time as you can. Pay attention to details that will allow you to detect the subtleties that often dictate why people do what they do.

Tables II, IV, and V show a wide range of needs, how each is manifested in a work-related scenario, the forces that control it, and corresponding motivational actions you should consider taking. These tables *cannot* describe the million and one nuances that can affect someone's needs. A person's behavior may not always fit into neat little, readily definable cubbyholes. To figure out some people, you have to look at them over time and make some preliminary motivational assumptions. Test those assumptions, observe what happens, and compare the results to the tables. Use your discoveries to repeat the process and test even more ambitious suppositions.

To show you how this works, make believe that some guy named Don was just hired as your new boss. All you know about Don is his reputation for sticking his nose into any activity that attracts the attention of top management. Will Don be any better than his predecessor? I don't know. Maybe he'll be worse, but you can do more than to just guess about him. Put him to the test and check him out.

Try something with Don. Suppose that you're working on a few high-profile projects. You need Don's help as much as you need canker sores, but invite him in anyway. Tell him you have things under control, but that a minor problem has arisen and you need his advice on it. Pick something you know he can solve in only a few minutes.

Don may also have a need to be respected or admired, so be prepared to test that possibility. Tell him you have sought his help because of his experience, his expertise, or perhaps his friendship with someone else whose help you need. Don't be obvious, but smear on the praise. See whether he bites. You can then keep it up, or shut up accordingly.

Assuming that he agrees to give you a hand, does he seem to be satisfied just to be working on the problem, or does he attempt to open the floodgates, jump to center stage, and take over? If you're not certain, thank him for his assistance and repeat the same tactics all over again several days later. This time, try a situation that would occupy his attention for few hours; perhaps even a few days. That will give you even more time to see what makes him tick.

Don may be unable to resist taking the credit for your hard work. You can't very well complain to anyone about that, but you can take advantage of it when a similar situation arises in the future. For Don to be happy, he has to be the hero, but does that mean the only hero? Test him on that.

The next time you do something, issue a report, sign it, and ask him to sign as the boss. Without being heavy-handed, use the body of the report to give him credit for something. If that pleases him, you know what to do from that point forward. If you're not sure, leave the next report on his desk with a note asking whether he wants it issued under his signature or yours.

What else does Don do? Is he fanatical about always having the last word? Will he be satisfied just to contend with others for success? Or does he get fulfilled only by destroying his competitors? These needs are often hard to distinguish from one another. Without a significant amount of evidence, you may find that distinctions between them are difficult to draw with confidence.

I'm not even going to try enumerating every conceivable need Don might have, but I can tell you that like everyone else on this earth, Don is probably driven most by fear, ego, or some combination of both. Do yourself a favor and develop a better appreciation for these emotions. The effort will make you that much better a motivator.

Table III. NEEDS

Person needs to	Behavior	Controlling Forces	Motivational Tactics
have a friend	Wants to share feelings/experiences	Fear of being alone	Invite him to join you for lunch. Share an experience with him. Ask him how he feels. Act like you care
be included	A compulsion to be a part of whatever is going on	Fear of being left out	Invite him to wherever the action is
be at the center of things	Calls meetings. Seeks to be heard, and to blow his own horn	Ego plus fear of being overshadowed by others	Suggest how he can be heard. Offer him a platform and perhaps also a megaphone
be the hero	Will tolerate no other heroes	Fear of being #2, not #1	Help him to be #1. Share your glory with him
control	Must have the last word. Authoritative. Leery of anyone unwilling to take his orders. Won't delegate	Ego and fear that others are inept. May feel inadequate, but won't admit it	The more you fight, the more he'll fight you. Show him you are an ally. Let him think he is in charge
compete	Win or lose, the fight is what counts as much as the outcome	Ambition	Suggest an opponent

win	Thrives on defeating others	Ambition/pride	Help him win.
hurt or destroy	Winning isn't good enough. He wants to harm or annihilate others	Anger or jealousy	Divert his wrath to someone else
have the last word	Must approve everything, no matter how minor. A bottleneck	Ego and fear of mistakes	Help him crush his enemies. Suggest a victim (not you)
be independent	Will not be controlled. May be aloof, arrogant	Ego plus fear of others who don't care about him	Don't box him in. Help him avoid being under anyone's control
be accepted	Hates to be rejected/embarrassed	Pride	Help him avoid being turned down
be left alone	Aloof. Friendly only if you initiate contact. Won't return calls	Fear of being interrupted or distracted	Be his hatchet man. Do the work that would otherwise distract him
be left alone	Aloof and standoffish. Few people know what this person wants or is doing. No team spirit	Fears he would lose his job and influence if others knew his "secrets"	May be difficult to reach unless he is your boss. Give him new secrets. Protect him from his enemies
deceive	Says one thing, does another. Makes offers that are too good to be true	Fears that honesty is weakness. His ego believes he can con anyone	Find him a target other than yourself. Be his hatchet man. Motivate him to put it in writing or on tape

Table IV. More Needs

Person needs to	Behavior	Controlling Forces	How to Motivate
go by the book	Hides behind rules, regulations	Fear	Find rules that buttress your viewpoint
blame others	Likes having scapegoats	Fear	Suggest victims other than yourself
have stability	Blocks new ideas	Fear of anything new	Show him how what seems new is actually quite similar to something that happened years ago with no adverse effects
be safe	Wants security in general	Fear	Eliminate or mitigate the cause of the fear
be safe	Wants others to take all the risks	Fear	Volunteer to take blame if things go wrong
be safe	Needs others to take care of him	Fear	Constant reassurances
be ridiculously safe	Any risk is an unacceptable risk. May have bunker mentality	Terror	If you can't get hurt, take the blame for his mistakes. Help him to feel safe
Avoid risk	Proceeds with caution	Prudence	Help him to identify and eliminate risks

be excited	Miserable if not enthused	Boredom	Give or suggest something new to do
be challenged	Is miserable if not confronted with interesting challenges	Boredom or burnout	Give or suggest something that's difficult but doable (no danger if he fails)
take risks	Seeks dangerous challenges. Thrives on pressure	Boredom or burnout, plus arrogance	Give or suggest something rather tough to do, with a penalty if he fails
move up	May want more power or something different to do	Ambition	Suggest ways to make a hit with his boss. Help him to make a good impression
achieve	Accomplishment	Pride	Suggest achievements he can reach
grow	Wants to learn and to become better at his job	Humility	Tell him stories from which he can learn. Diplomatically point out his own mistakes
enjoy	Wants to have fun at work	Intelligence; he's the smartest of all	Find out what he enjoys the most and help him to do it more often
be praised	Needs frequent compliments	Fear	Shovel on the flattery
make money	Strictly mercenary	Ambition/Greed	Suggest ways to make a hit with his boss. Help him to make a good impression
give	Wants to return a favor	Gratitude	Suggest who to thank and how to do it
take	Always wants more	Greed	Suggest how he can get something in return for what he will perceive as nothing

Table V. STILL MORE NEEDS

Person likes	Behavior	Motivate By
fine clothes, careful grooming	Looks good; likes others who look good	praising his looks without gushing; looking good yourself
neatness	Can't stand messiness	hiding your mess; helping him clean up
timeliness	3 P.M. means between 2:59 and 3:01	being prompt and being precise when you make commitments involving time
small talk	Chatty	listening
no small talk	All business. Won't be drawn into small talk	shutting up and listening
loyalty	Appreciates your seeming to put him first. Wants to know that you see his needs as more important than anyone else's	telling him what he wants to hear
someone to listen to him	May not start the small talk, but will respond if you start it	asking how he is feeling. If you know his family, ask about them. Otherwise, by listening, but not being judgmental; making him feel comfortable in talking with you

subordinates those who stay late	Big ego and need to control means more concern with how late you stay than with how much you do	putting in an occasional after hours appearance, making sure he sees you
being told about his mistakes	Wants to improve himself	being honest and forthright
never being wrong	Never accepts blame	suggesting scapegoats, or being one if you can without getting hurt
not being interrupted	Wants attention	shutting up and waiting for him to finish
playing as much as working	Wants to have fun	letting him, joining him
talking about his outside interests	Looking for a kindred soul	acting as if you have the same interests
talking about his family	Brags about his kids	telling him how great they are

FEAR

You can deal with the fears people feel about potentially losing their jobs, their power, their reputation, or their ability to meet career goals. Motivation is often a matter of calming these fears and helping people to overcome them. If you can do neither, you must revert to a Plan B that convinces people that you are the reason why their biggest on-the-job fears will shortly go away.

Tread lightly. People do not want to be told that their fears have rendered them emotionally paralyzed or ineffectual. They may be insulted if you state or suggest that they are afraid. Instead, say that you think they are prudent. To be prudent is to be wise and careful, which is a lot better than being stupid. Using *prudent* implies that you appreciate and understand their predicament and their thinking.

Having convinced your prey that you do not find them fearful, you can then try discovering what they are so damned afraid of. Testing for fears can be risky, however, if all you have going for you are raw courage and the information shown here in Tables III through V. You won't do yourself any favors by offering scapegoats or words of praise to people who want words of loyalty.

This is where testing comes in. Be as supportive and nonthreatening as you can be at first, and *observe* as closely as you can. If you suspect that fear is a problem, take an educated guess as to what scares the person. Be as precise as possible. At first, test your guess in a small way, and then in bigger ways until you are able to confirm what motivation is required. When you find out what that is, don't pass judgment on it. Accept it and use your knowledge of it to make the other person feel better about you.

EGO

Fear is probably the single most important motivational factor, but ego is a close second. Spotting someone with an excess of ego is not difficult. Arrogant and self-centered, the egotist thinks of himself as an expert in all areas. No matter what your area of specialization is, egocentric people think they know (or can quickly learn) more about it than you know.

Independent and resentful of authority, egotists work themselves hard, and they relentlessly push their subordinates. Although none of them are perfect, many of them actually are as smart as they think they are. You might find their personalities not to your taste, but don't be deceived; some of them can pour on loads of charm when they have to motivate someone they can't dominate.

Describing egocentric people is the easy part. The hard part is figuring out how to deal with them. If the characteristics I have just described seem familiar, they belong to the typical CEO. As much as you may or may not like them, you can't just dismiss dictatorial executives as deranged control freaks who happen to be in power. They do want control, but they are not demented. They *are* important to your career, and you should take them seriously. You can learn more about them in chapter 7.

WHEN IN ROME

A great way to figure out how to handle someone is to look at the people he trusts and depends on. Who are they? How do they treat him? What do they offer to meet his needs? Do they do his dirty work? Run errands for him? Tell him only what he wants to hear? Stay late at work every night so he thinks he is getting a lot of work from them?

You can answer these questions in three steps:

1. Note who successfully handles him.
2. Figure out what they do that brings them their success with him.
3. Do what they do.

Several years ago I attended an outdoor music festival concert along with some twenty thousand other Beethoven fans. As we all left the unpaved parking area shortly before 11 P.M., traffic slowed to a crawl. A mile or so ahead of me, however, one car broke out of line and drove off the gravel road. I had no idea where the driver thought he was going, but he seemed to be heading toward the outside main road. Within seconds, another eight to ten cars were right behind him. They were moving right along, while the rest of us were sitting still. I was just about to pull out of line to follow them, when they suddenly stopped. Some of them—actually most of them—then turned around and got back in line behind me. What happened? The lead car and the two right behind him had driven into a swamp. They couldn't see it, and once they got in, they had to be towed out!

How do you stay on the right path and avoid swamps? You can and you should observe those ahead of you. What have the successful ones done? How do they differ from the "never weres" or the "also rans"? But don't just follow. Keep your eyes open and test the better possibilities as best you can before you commit yourself in any one direction.

CIRCUMSTANCES

No one acts one way all day, every day. Each of us may typically behave in one manner or another, but we are likely to
change our ways markedly depending on our mood and on
the situations in which we find ourselves. Someone who is
usually calm and even-tempered when things are going well,
for example, may be high strung and difficult to work with if
he thinks his job, reputation, or happiness is on the line.

Consider the person you want to motivate, and note what
happens when circumstances place him under unusual and
sudden pressures. How does he usually react to being blind-
sided by unexpected problems? Does he become more
impetuous or more cautious? What did he do the last time a
similar thing happened? Did he go to anyone for advice?
Who? What was he told to do? How did he respond? What
did everyone else do? Taken together with his normal fears,
the answers to these questions will give you clues to his nature
when the heat is on him.

If your luck is anything like mine, however, the circumstances you need may not come along by themselves with a
regularity or an intensity that suits your purposes. If that happens, or if your local circumstance store is closed, perhaps
you can create a few of your own.

............6............

Make Your Own Luck

Bosses can be milked for much, if not most, of what you want from your job, but only if you capitalize on every one of the numerous opportunities they will present to you for meeting their needs. That's right; they'll *give* you opportunities, and plenty of them. Basic human needs manifest themselves as a nonstop series of compulsions that bosses feel all day long, not just when they ask you to do something.

You can't possibly make the most of an opportunity, however, unless you first recognize it, and you certainly won't do that if you're daydreaming or doing anything else that has your mind performing at less than full capacity. Your mind cannot shift from stupidity to brilliance in the blink of an eye. If you allow it to tune out when you are bored or uninterested, how will you react when an opportunity comes your way? Will you be able to capitalize on it? I don't think so. You probably won't even see it.

LUCK

At various times in your life, you have no doubt met people you consider lucky. You know the type; they escape without a scratch from disasters that would cripple the rest of us. Good things are always happening for them. This is particularly true in the area of job satisfaction, where so-called "lucky" people seem to get all the choice assignments, raises, promotions, preferential treatment, and other good breaks.

In my experience, none of this happens by chance. You can bet that the people to whom I refer are given nothing free of charge, that they work hard for what they get, and that much of their "luck" stems from identifying and capitalizing on opportunities. Upon finding an opportunity they like, they pounce on it, and *then* they get "lucky." In other words, they make their own luck.

Don't be jealous of them or angry at them for getting all the goodies you want. That's the wrong focus. To get the right focus, do what they do. Find opportunities in everything that occurs, and create opportunities when nothing happens. That's what "luck" is all about.

OPPORTUNISM

Envision your boss asking you to return a report she loaned you several days ago. You pick it up and take it to her office, where you find her talking to someone. Not wanting to interrupt, you unobtrusively get her attention and drop the report on her desk. Isn't that what she asked you to do?

Yes, that's what *she* asked of you, but you can do more than that. If you want money, career mobility, responsibility, greater freedom to implement your ideas, or other rewards that only she can give you, use the opportunity to your advantage. Plan ahead, think about the report, and focus on your goals. How can you meet your needs by meeting her needs?

Before you bring that report to her, skim through it for a few minutes. Remind yourself what it says, particularly in light of what you know about her views. Then, be sure to return the report only if you have a chance to speak to her about it. If she is with someone else when you arrive, come back later when she is alone. Hand her the report, but don't just leave. Pick a topic about which the report agrees with her, and say that you were glad to see the way it dealt with that topic. Do not point out that the report confirms her thinking; that would be too conspicuous. The trick is to make her believe that it confirms *your* thinking.

Alternatively, pick out a point of view contrary to hers and say that the report has erred on that matter. Don't say it disagreed with her; say it goofed. Don't do it in a big way, don't dwell on it, don't attempt to engage her in an extended conversation, and don't make yourself obvious by saying "I agree with you." Let *her* come to that conclusion. Just make your comment in an offhand manner and leave.

By following this path, you don't just merely return a report, you create the perception that your views align with hers. This in turn will indicate to her that the two of you are on the same side—at least on one particular issue—and therefore you are more likely to be an ally than a threat.

As you have probably already figured out by yourself, careers are not made or destroyed on the basis of incidents like the one I have just described. There's only so much you can do to capitalize on returning a report, and the benefit to you for pulling it off is indeed small. Although the benefits from any one opportunity may be insignificant, small political benefits add up to major gains in the same way that even the largest dollar amounts can be paid in pennies. You might not prefer it that way, but you'd be a fool not to take your opportunities any way you can find them. Make the most of those small opportunities, and someday you'll be able to bank on them.

If you keep up to date with the news on television, radio, newspapers, or trade magazines, you can't help every so often coming across something that relates to the place where you work, its industry, its customers, or even its management. An item of interest could be anything from a story about new tax laws to a report on something new that a competitor has developed.

Suppose you find such an item. Do you read it and do nothing other than tell yourself, "That's interesting"? I hope that isn't all you do. Why not capitalize on it? You could, for example, write a little memo to the boss on the subject. The boss will hopefully then perceive you as a concerned employee who is also the conveyor of valuable news.

That would be better than nothing, but anybody can write that type of memo—and lots of people do. To leap all over that news item and make it yours, not only should you tell the boss what it is, but also what should be done about it. Tell him, "Here's what I think we should do...," give him an action plan, and make certain that plan addresses *his* fears, *his* ego drives, and all *his* other needs.

This is what I mean by opportunism—making your own luck by taking simple situations and turning them into motivational opportunities that you turn to your advantage. Many everyday occurrences can be turned into such opportunities, but only if they are properly exploited.

A SHOULDER TO LEAN ON

Make yourself available to motivate people by showing a willingness to listen to them in their times of need. Pressure on them means opportunity for you; identify it and make something of it. Whether it's staying late, coming in on the weekend, or getting together for lunch, look for signs that "a shoulder to lean on" or "an ear to bend" would be welcome. Don't wait to be asked. Act now and show your availability.

But what if you don't know how or when to direct your help? Should you guess? No more than you have to. Misplaced help or offers of help may be unwelcome and might be seen as presumptuous or as meddling in areas that are none of your business. Assuming for the moment that your boss is the person you wish to motivate, watch his facial expressions, words, and demeanor when he gets off the telephone, comes out of a meeting, or reads a letter. Has he recently been hit with new demands such as tight deadlines, customer problems, or news of impending layoffs? Has he taken on new responsibilities?

If nothing happens that you can see, and yet he looks or acts worried or hurried, ask him what's wrong, but do it unobtrusively:

Is everything okay?

If the response you get is a question as to why you are asking that, say "You look worried, that's all." He will either give you an answer you can use, or he'll clam up. If he says nothing, drop it. If he *does* tell you what is bothering him, figure out what he would need to feel better about the situation, and help him to get it. Don't limit yourself to helping him with work-related problems. He may say he had to take a bus to work this morning because his car is in the shop. That's great! Offer him a ride home.

CREATING OPPORTUNITIES

Some opportunities exist only because you make them exist. One way to do this would be to break something so you could become a hero by fixing it, but that's demented and I certainly don't recommend it. If you were to create the perception of a problem, however, who better than you could solve it?

When Ted Stewart was my boss, I was planning to make a presentation to a potentially huge customer who had never before done business with us. Millions of dollars were on the line. Our strength was that we were first to market with remotely accessible pollution monitors. We needed a way to make the most of our technology, and I suggested videotaped interviews with satisfied customers. The problem with that was that we had no video camera, no VCR, and not even a TV set in the office.

A bigger problem was Ted himself. He was terrified of losing business to anyone else, but he was also cheap. Our customers were spread all across the country, and even if we did the editing ourselves, the travel cost for my little scheme would have been ten to fifteen thousand dollars. Ted vetoed the idea.

Then word reached me that this customer had been offered a guided tour of our competitor's new research laboratory. Brand X had spent millions on that lab, and ours couldn't hold up to theirs. I went right back to Ted, making the case that his option was *not* to save ten thousand, but to spend it or lose out on millions. He may not have liked that, but I got to buy the video equipment and a pocketful of plane tickets. Three months later, we got the order. That he liked.

Ted was a sucker for creative ways of appealing to his fears, but he isn't the only one. To do the same with other people, create a motivational opportunity by capitalizing on the other person's fears and sell your point of view by giving him a choice with all the cards stacked in your favor. You may think his fears are ridiculous, but an opportunity is an opportunity, so don't let it escape you!

After observing your boss in action for some time, learn to recognize the types of situations that cause him to worry. If he recently suffered losses because certain customers didn't pay their bills, for example, anticipate his fears the next time you land a new account. Hand him a credit report on the customer before he has a chance to ask for it. You'll make his life easier. Make a habit of taking his fears into account and he'll learn to appreciate you. If he's a punctuality nut, for example, don't make him wait.

But don't think only in terms of his fears. Think also about what he likes. Italian restaurants? Airplane seats on the aisle? A certain brand of wine? These things are easy to notice, easy to list, and easy to get. Without being obvious, make sure he has them and that he knows you got them for him.

SCHMOOZING

You know Frank has teenage children, but as you stand there in his office waiting for him to get off the phone, you realize you would have never expected them to be that ugly. Yet there they are, in living color, right over there in that ghastly new photograph on his desk. That must be his wife with them. No wonder the kids look so strange.

What does this have to do with increasing your job satisfaction? Nothing, if you can't get past your own narrow tastes and opinions. The important point to notice is not whether you like the way they look. By placing the picture in a prominent place, Frank is telling you that *he* likes the way they look. His family probably means a great deal to him, which means that you may be able to put him in an agreeable mood by getting him to focus on them. So what if they look like mutants? That's his problem, but he has just hung up, which is your problem. Don't be obvious and tell him how pretty or handsome his kids are; capitalize on the situation by saying:

**"Looks like you're going to have two in college
at the same time pretty soon."**

With those seemingly innocent words, you have engaged him in conversation on a subject he enjoys. No, Frank won't enjoy paying for two college educations at once, but fathers do love to talk about their children. He may not say a lot about them, but he will say something. Once he does (*"That's right, my oldest starts next year."*), you may be able to say something else (*"Where is she thinking of going?"*) and motivate him to talk even more.

You may or may not be able to take the conversation too much further, but your objective here is to make Frank feel good by helping him meet his need to brag about his kids. If you have accomplished that much, you may have him in the mood to talk in detail about his needs.

What you are doing here is *schmoozing,* cleverly using small talk to accomplish some aim other than to pass the time. The purpose of schmoozing is to get someone to feel comfortable with you and to open up to you—even if just a little—so you can figure out what turns him on or off and how you can best motivate him.

Remember the boss whose car was being repaired? I'm going to assume you did give him a ride home. Maybe his car wasn't ready and you volunteered transportation for the following day as well. Once he is in your vehicle, he's a captive audience. Be an opportunist. Schmooze with the man. Tell him about the last time you had car problems. Having an experience in common with him may help him to feel better about you. Better yet, use the car story to open a dialogue and then ask him how things are going on some project you know is close to his heart. Listen carefully and he will probably give you one if not several clues as to how you can motivate him.

Here's another example. You're going downstairs for a meeting when Bill Ward, the corporate director of marketing, gets on the elevator with you. You know Bill, but you can't stand him on a personal level. He's offensive, he's crude, and being exposed to his breath reminds you of the last time you were in a barn.

Focus past all that. You'd like to move into marketing and Bill is the person you must impress to get there. You have no other choice. Forget that he's personally disgusting. You don't have to kiss the pig, you have to schmooze with him. But what do you do—ask him for a transfer? Yes, but not on the elevator. You won't have the time. Never squander an opportunity to start a conversation you won't be able to finish in the privacy that the situation may call for.

Use the meeting on the elevator to establish rapport. Try to bring up a topic that came up the last time you had any dealings with him. Maybe he mentioned some market research at that point. Ask him if the survey results came in. Be specific so he knows what survey results you mean, but don't be demanding, and inquire about the survey as if your interest were purely professional. Perceiving you to have interests in common with his own, he'll probably be happy to tell you all about those results. When he's doing that, ask him for a few minutes in his office to discuss a "personal" matter. He'll probably be glad to oblige.

As was the case with most political maneuvers, schmoozing cannot be expected to result in instant, sweeping changes. A minute on the elevator will not rocket you to the top of the organizational chart. It may, however, put you in a favorable light in the eyes of those who are already there.

LISTENING

Every human being occasionally feels a need for someone to talk to. This is also true of the many corporate executives who have fallen for the old adage about life being lonely at the top. If their egos are sufficiently bloated, bosses well below the top behave the same way. Not only do they have to live with the pressures of doing their jobs and managing their careers, they subject themselves to the added pressure of hiding their feelings behind a confident but phony facade. This is bad for them and also good for you, if it results in their being moody and unpredictable.

Schmoozing meets a basic human need we all have to share our burdens and talk about our problems with the aim of gaining empathy, if not assistance. People do want to talk. What keeps them from completely spilling their guts are two old friends: fear and ego. Fear is involved because they don't want to look weak or inept, and ego gets into the act because they instinctively hate to admit needing anything from anybody.

For schmoozing to work, you have to perfect an ability I described in chapter 1: listening. This is tougher than you might think. Most people listen only to what they want to hear, but you must avoid that. Focus on what the other person is trying to say. This would be easy if everybody were articulate, but most people are anything but good communicators. No matter how much education they have, their vocabulary may be limited, they may habitually choose ambiguous terminology, and they may even select confusing words.

You can't force people to improve their communication skills. For you to understand what they are thinking, you may first have to provoke other people to talk, and that may require a considerable amount of schmoozing. If you are successful in starting a conversation, don't just hear the words that are being spoken to you. Listen to them and critically interpret their meaning. Look at the other person's facial expressions. What is his tone of voice telling you? How are his circumstances affecting him? The individual who tells you nothing is wrong may be troubled with worry, fear, or anger.

To make schmoozing a little easier, try the following:

- Stimulate conversation by asking questions that can't be answered with a *yes* or a *no*.
- If you don't know much about a subject that someone enjoys discussing, commiserate with him on a problem you both have or used to have. Other possibilities are to ask about mutual friends or something at the forefront of the news.
- Avoid political or religious topics unless you are certain of the other person's beliefs. You don't want to upset the guy; you want to make him feel comfortable enough to open up to you.
- If he does start to talk, shut up and let him finish. Don't interrupt.
- If he seems to have run out of things to say, ask a question to clarify something he said previously. If he has told a story, ask him what happened next.

- Use restatement as another tool to get him to say more. After he tells you about having been given a difficult time by an important customer, you can say "You mean he actually threw our catalog on the floor?" He may proceed to bore you with the same stupid story all over again, but that's good. He'll do that only if he is comfortable talking with you.
- Do not argue.
- Laugh with him, never at him, and only when he is clearly trying to be funny.
- Do not frown or show any other sign that you doubt him or the validity of what he is saying.
- Unless you are trying to show astonishment or surprise at what he is telling you, smile while he is talking.
- Look attentive, stare right between his eyes, and punctuate that stare only with an occasional head nod and "Uh huh, really?", "I see," or "You don't say." An exclamation such as "What a shame!" or "That stinks!" may also be appropriate if he is describing some injustice he had to endure.
- When you reply, empathize with any problems he describes, but not in such a way that creates the perception of trying to outdo him.
- Remember that you are *not* a district attorney and that he is *not* a defendant. Ask questions to clarify what he is saying, not to interrogate him.
- Be leery of anyone who will not look at you when speaking but instead glances everyplace else in the room. This *may* be a sign that the person is lying.
- Know when to stop. Pay attention to the person with whom you are talking. Is he looking at his watch, fidgeting, staring at his work, typing on his computer while you talk, putting on his coat, or walking toward the door? Zip your lips immediately if you see any of those signs.

People will love you if you tell them that they have been the victim of rotten breaks, that they can certainly overcome the problems now facing them, and that they can always count on you. They may want more than that, but be careful. Some people appreciate repeated assistance or commiseration only if they ask for it.

STROKING

You find out that your boss is a photography nut. Knick-knacks, magazines, and other evidence to that effect are all over the office. You think that the whole camera scene is only slightly less exciting than watching grass grow, but he doesn't have to know that. Approach him when he's not bearing down on you for anything; ideally when you have just done something he wanted, and preferably right after he's paid you a compliment. Say that you have been thinking of taking up photography, and that you'd appreciate any advice he could give you on how to get started. He may seem unresponsive, but if he thinks you are sincere, don't be surprised if he answers you in an uncharacteristically friendly tone of voice.

If my photography example is not applicable, what else might he enjoy? Fishing? Boating? Tennis? Stamp collecting? Golf? The leading team in baseball, football, or hockey? How about gardening or carpentry? He must have some outside interests.

Look around his office for clues, and listen carefully to his conversation. If you can't come up with anything, perhaps his job is more than his work. Maybe it's also his hobby. If he is the founder of the company, ask him how he started the business. An alternative would be to ask him how he got his job or chose his profession.

This is what I call *stroking;* making someone perceive that you look up to him. If you can make that happen, you will meet his need to be esteemed for his talent or other personal attributes, not just because he is your boss. At the same time, he will appreciate your giving him the chance to pontificate.

Forget about overwhelming evidence to the contrary. So what if his latest idea is wasting millions of dollars? As long as the company has enough left over for what you feel is your fair share, what do you care? You've already tried logic on him and all you got for your trouble was a severe reprimand. Next time you approach him, tell him only what he wants to hear. Use stroking to make his ego feel good about you.

If you can't stroke in any other way, try appearance. An opportunity may present itself the next time your boss returns from the beauty salon. This woman doesn't need a new hairdo; she needs a new face. You'd have to be a warthog to find her attractive, but that's the truth only as you perceive it. She probably sees it differently. You'll lose if you try to convince her that your truth is more valid than hers. If you focus only on maximizing your job satisfaction, on the other hand, you'll submerge the urge to smirk, focus on her need to be admired, and tell her how great she looks.

Just don't overdo it. There's a fine line between stroking and patronizing, and you should never patronize anyone. People might see right through your little deception, and become offended at what you are trying to do. Don't pay too many compliments at any one time, don't gush, and don't underestimate anyone's intelligence. A person's egocentric tendencies make him vulnerable, not stupid.

OFFERING SCAPEGOATS

The goal in stroking people is to put their fears at rest, gratify their egos, and make them feel good. A person for whom things have gone wrong will find stroking particularly welcome. He may blame himself, but not in your presence. You will see only that he's in a lousy mood, is sulking, and is apt to lash out in anger at any handy target.

Then you arrive on the scene. Sensing the nature of the situation, wanting very much to seize the moment and capitalize on an opportunity to make the boss happy, you suggest a scapegoat on whom to blame the company's problems. Ideally, such a scapegoat must meet two criteria: it, he, she, or them must plausibly be at fault, but unable to refute your charges. A competitor, government auditor, or former employee would be perfect. A product or supplier might also work, if its claims can be disputed.

You may object to blaming others for your mistakes. If so, I commend you for having qualities that are quite scarce these days: honesty and integrity. Unlike diamonds and other rare commodities, however, these qualities aren't worth much in the corporate world nowadays. Tell most bosses the truth and they'll get angry, perhaps even at you for reminding them of reality. Tell them only what they want to hear, however, and they'll let nothing stop them from being nice to you.

Corporate CEOs love having hundreds, if not thousands, of scapegoats. This is precisely what they create for themselves during layoffs. The truth about most downsizings is that they stem from mistakes in sales and profit projections and their associated staffing requirements. Regardless of which company, institution, or government agency is involved, however, all these mistakes—100 percent of them—have one thing in common: they were made at the top of the organizational food chain. None were committed at the bottom.

Yet, when things are not going well, the folks at the bottom are asked to pay the price for the problems created by the folks at the top. For refusing to be slaves and having the audacity to take a salary that drains the corporate coffers, the troops in the trenches bear all the pain of the typical corporate restructuring. They are downsized out the door at the first sign of trouble. What about the CEO who completely screwed up, misread projections, and failed to see that he was hiring too many people? Don't worry about him. Displaying a flood of crocodile tears for the newly unemployed, he'll give himself a raise and stay on to make more blunders.

Without seeming presumptuous or otherwise out of line, you can't actually tell a boss to blame scapegoats for his problems. What you can do is to name names and let them draw his own conclusions. For example, you might say:

> *"This would have never happened if Jones hadn't opened up his mouth about…"*

> *or*

> *"The damn software didn't work the way they said it would."*

Add an additional sentence or two to buttress your point, and stop. Will your suggestion be taken? You may never know, but by shifting blame to a scapegoat, you stroke the person whose mood you wish to improve. That person most assuredly does not wish to get mad at himself, and he may feel that he would be seen as self-serving if he did the scapegoat naming. By doing that for him, you have done him a favor. If he knows that, you have done yourself a favor, too.

NO PROBLEMS, PLEASE. JUST SOLUTIONS.

Don't bring problems to a boss. Bring him solutions. Bosses
don't like problems. If you can't solve problems, their little
minds may tell them, *you* are a problem and should be
thrown out. Why should they put up with you when they
could instead hire someone who brings them solutions?

Before you go to your boss for help on what to do in the
face of a dilemma, do nothing. Stop and think. Turn that
problem into an opportunity to show how valuable you are in
terms of making the boss's life easier. Even if you don't know
what to do, surely you can come up with a plan that will lead
you in the right direction. Put your plan on paper, and work
out the details. *Then* go to your leader for a go-ahead. Show
him how your ideas will make him look good, consolidate his
power, or accomplish something else that turns him on. If you
don't need his approval, solve the problem on your own,
immediately pumping up the volume to show how much you
have done to meet his needs.

CHOOSE YOUR BATTLES

Being available for bosses and helping them in times of need
are effective ways to motivate, but do not expect your efforts
to speak for themselves, by themselves. You have to make
sure they are noticed *and* that you get the credit for them.
Coming in two hours early to have things all ready for the
boss's trip is going to make him happy, but it won't do you a
bit of good unless he knows that you did it.

Can you tell him that you did it? Yes, but don't tell him
why. Avoid bragging, saying anything that might be perceived

as arrogant, or giving the impression that you did what you did because you thought you would profit from it. The same situations that offer opportunities to enhance job satisfaction also give you opportunities to make a fool of yourself, perhaps to impose a serious setback on your career. If you push too hard to do too much politically inspired motivating too quickly and/or too obviously, you may be seen as a self-promoter and a phony who should not be trusted.

People will like you if they perceive you as an asset they can rely on to meet their needs, but that doesn't mean they want you hovering about at all hours of the day and night. If they tire of you or see through your intentions, they'll want no more of you. Rather than smothering a person with your help and doing your career more harm than good, you should carefully pick and choose the best opportunities, and the best ways of blowing your own horn. If you'll lose nothing by letting the next opportunity pass, perhaps that's exactly what you should do. Something else will soon appear to take its place.

In a more general sense, you don't have to try to hit a home run every time an opportunity arises. Attempt to capitalize only when you have something to say, when you can meet a known need, when what you do say will not backfire on you, and when you are certain of not being obvious. In other words, your goal at bat should be to connect with the ball, not just to swing hard and fan the air.

·············7··············

Under Siege

Tyrannical bosses are a fact of life in many a corporate hierarchy. For many of us, reporting to them is the most difficult aspect of getting job satisfaction. Slightly conceited if not totally egomaniacal, they are domineering, remote, and typically difficult if not impossible to question, much less work with.

What sets corporate dictators apart from the rest of us is their fanaticism about pursuing what they want, and their willingness to do almost anything to force the rest of us into complying with their demands. They have no reservations about catching us off guard, putting us on the defensive, and keeping us there by yelling, berating, threatening, and pressuring us without letup.

Some of them are quite aware that the more we fear them, the more likely we will be to fall into line when they make demands, and the less able we will be to threaten their security or coerce them when we want something. Others are so self-absorbed that their actions are instinctive. Thinking only of themselves, they see us as conduits or obstacles to their goals. The fuel that drives them is ego. The bigger their ego, the greater their self-assurance and singlemindedness, and the more vulnerable they are to effective back-scratching.

Let's try to keep those egos happy. If we fail at that, let's at least divert their attention long enough for us to regroup and try a different approach. Here's how.

TAKE A STAND ON PRINCIPLE

Popular opinion is that arguing with dictatorial bosses will result in your head being severed, but that's a myth. The worst they are likely to do is to fire you, but they won't chew your head off. Maybe your nose, but not your head. And they probably won't fire you either.

You certainly can and should ask tough bosses any question about your job, your instructions, or your future. "Can I ask you a question?" however, may get "no" or "not right now" for an answer. If you have something to ask, ask it! As long as you request answers rather than demand them, you will probably get them.

Do you push your luck and inquire further to figure out why the boss has made such an apparently lamebrained decision? Sure, but do it the right way, not the wrong way. Quarreling with bosses is always possible, but only under two conditions:

- if you convince them that your goals are the same as theirs, and
- if you refrain from attacking their wisdom, their honesty, their freedom to do as they see fit, or their abilities.

Challenge someone's decisions and opinions all you like, but not their intelligence. Never tell the egotist or anyone else that he is wrong.

A wiser alternative is to take a stand on principle. Begin by mentioning any points on which you agree with him. Say that you're impressed by the thought that went into his position. Instead of disagreeing with that position, however, tout your own point of view. But don't stop there. Back yourself up, preferably with facts other than the ones he used in reaching his conclusions. Explain his position by claiming that he was misinformed, misled, or given incomplete information—but not stupid.

You may know he was stupid, but remember: Perceptions count more than facts, and focusing on someone's stupidity or other weaknesses will provoke his ego to turn on you. By paying a few compliments, and by not insulting him, you keep his ego quiet and you give it no excuse for getting bent out of shape.

The next time you find yourself getting sucked into a dispute with someone who is heavy on ego and light on motivation for letting you win, ask yourself what you would gain by going to battle with this person. Would you get a lucrative book deal? Prizes and cash awards? Huge speaking fees? You know better than that. If your only gain would be to win the battle and prove that you can get your way with him, be careful. That would be a gain for your ego, but at what cost? If the boss's ego gets mad because it perceives that you are insulting his intelligence, you may well lose a great deal more than the stupid argument.

MEANWHILE, BACK AT THE BUNKER

One of the more difficult people to work with is someone whose fear and ego drive him in seemingly equal proportions. This guy is so self-centered that thinking other than his own is highly alien to him. He can't believe that anyone else's ideas are as good as his, and he thinks well of us only if we agree with him. If you question his wisdom or interfere with his plans, he'll explode at you. To make things worse, he is quite paranoid, and he may extrapolate reality to the point where he thinks that you are *always* threatening him. If that's the case, he'll always be furious with you.

In the extreme case, he'll develop the "bunker" mentality. This is a condition in which he thinks that everybody is against him, that every event is a source of bad news, that no one can be trusted, and that he must put up a wall of defenses to ward off the evil forces conspiring against him. The only people allowed within that wall are his trusted henchmen.

He'll jump down your throat with both feet at the slightest hint that your loyalty is in doubt, but your loyalty will definitely be in doubt if you ever have the audacity to question his thinking. Unbelievably cautious, the only thing he'll do in a hurry is criticize people who can't fight back, such as subordinates. Someplace in the back of his mind he may even hope they'll argue with him. That way, he can rebuke them and yell at them, thus showing everyone else (and his ego) that he is still powerful.

Instead of worrying about whether fear or ego predominates with this character, the trick in dealing with him is to recognize him for what he is, and to become one of his henchmen. You do not have to be male to do this. You have to make him feel safe and comfortable. Start by heaping on the praise, saying nasty things about his enemies, feeding him an endless supply of scapegoats to blame when he fails, and showing him your loyalty by never seeming to tire of listening to his rantings.

Talk in a way that calms him, not one that frightens him. If you must change his mind on something, position yourself as bringing up the point only to provide him with more security. But don't frame your argument that way; he'd be offended by the truth. Frame your argument around making everybody in the company more secure.

The boss in a bunker must perceive that you are a person on whom he can rely to help him ward off attacks from those who would question his wisdom or threaten to question it. Once you have met his needs better than anyone else, he will treat you better than he treats anyone else. It's that simple.

SELF-DEFENSE

The boss comes storming out of his office bellowing your name. He's infuriated at something you did and he just can't wait for the thrill of terrorizing you and peeling off your hide for some transgression he claims you have committed. If you meet him head on and challenge his accusations, you will end up the loser, so I recommend that you adopt any of the following tactics. At the least, they will allow you time to collect your thoughts. If you become skilled at using these schemes, you may actually be able to capitalize on your predicament and gain control of it.

Convince him that the damage is small. Show him that the situation he's so mad about is not a problem and does not interfere with his plans or his ability to meet his goals. Don't imply that he is exaggerating, but show him that you have always had a contingency plan for dealing with the matter.

Beat a strategic retreat. In its simplest form, a strategic retreat is just a matter of waiting for the right opportunity rather than trying to forge ahead when the odds are against you. If your boss is angry, for example, it might be smart to wait for him to mellow out before you make a move. I say "might" because if you tend to be tentative, you can easily retreat for weeks or months before summoning up the guts to go ahead. If you must retreat to wait for a break in the clouds, do so only temporarily.

Another variation of the strategic retreat is the draw play. That's a football move in which one team lets the other side rush straight in only to find that the quarterback has already gone someplace else. In the office version of the draw play, you don't argue with the onrushing boss, you don't get defensive, and you don't make excuses for whatever it is that he's distressed about.

Don't tell him to calm down, either. That might aggravate him even more. Instead, say that you don't blame him for feeling the way he does. Say that you were just on your way to give him the news yourself. Make it clear that not only do you admit culpability, you have already taken steps to recoup so that he suffers no losses. Of course your position will be stronger if you can rattle off a list of those steps.

Your objective in coming clean like this is to catch him by surprise. By offering no fight and by telling him that you have anticipated his needs, you will take the air right out of his sails, so to speak. He will have built up a big head of steam with which to beat you over the head, and he'll have no place to go with that steam.

Blame scapegoats. Don't let the poor man stand there fuming. Give him a target at which he can vent his fury. Explain that the whole mess wasn't entirely your fault and that you would never have done what you did if some idiot hadn't given you the wrong information or failed to provide some assistance you were counting on.

Be careful about telling the boss that he is your scapegoat of the hour. He may have said to you that the meeting was at 3 P.M., but if you show up at that hour only to be told you are thirty minutes late, don't blame him for your tardiness. Simply reply, *"I thought somebody said the meeting was at three."* He does not want to hear that he was the one who screwed up.

This last example illustrates use of a person I call the stealth scapegoat. It's easy to cast blame, but if you don't want to destroy careers or make enemies, say that you don't know (or don't remember) who was responsible for giving you the wrong input.

Restate and/or ask for clarification. Asking an egocentric individual to repeat and clarify his requests or viewpoints will often be helpful. He may be so focused on his own thinking that it never occurs to him that his original statement confused anyone else. Demanding an explanation would be counterproductive, but you can respond to him by opening with a preface like "Let me get this straight" or "Let me make sure I understand you" and then asking a clarification question:

> *"Wait a second. Are you saying that…?"*

You know what he meant, but he doesn't know that. The weakness of this example is that it can be quickly answered with a "yes" or "no." To get even more of his time, ask a clarification question that requires a more elaborate answer:

"How did that happen?"

or

"What leads you to believe that?"

or

"Why is that a problem?"

or

"What should I have done?"

When he asks a probing question, on the other hand, answering may be a little less painful if you can answer with a question of your own:

"Which deadline?"

or even

"No, but did you see my memo on that subject?"

Remember that to ask is not to cross-examine. The idea is not to pressure anyone, but to show concern and interest in a way that helps you gain more information. Asking clarification questions is also a great way to blunt questions you did not expect. Such questions won't get divert an attack, but they can interrupt the other person's train of thought and take away his momentum. Rather then blurting out an answer you may later regret, feigning a need for clarification has the added benefit of giving you a few extra seconds to prepare a response.

BRING UP THE RESERVES

Your boss comes up with the most asinine idea since the invention of the necktie. How do you react? Dare you be honest? Should you ask him to tell you which flea market he patronized to get his brain cells? You know better than that. The smart thing here is to think quickly and determine what would happen—not to the company, to you—if he got his way. So what if it would cause the company to squander a fortune? Would you be substantially penalized? If you would, take a stand on principle. If not, don't get angry about the situation. Focus on your goals and take advantage of it.

You may want to ask your chief some inoffensive questions about his idea, and perhaps inquire about some of his assumptions, but do that only briefly and then stop. Even if you could unleash some powerful arguments against his position, hold them in reserve. Tell him only that his idea is great, and then change the subject.

After a short but discreet interval, go back to him. Say that you understand how he reached his opinion, but that you want to ask some questions you hadn't thought of earlier. Another possibility is to tell him that you have new information that was not available to either of you earlier. He doesn't have to know that you are merely bringing up your reserves and implementing Plan B.

By holding your strongest arguments in reserve, you get to present them in a way that has been rehearsed, and perfected. By giving him an out, such as not having been told the full story in the first place, you let his ego off the hook.

Maybe you did *not* know what to say earlier. Perhaps you were so dumbfounded at the stupidity of his brainstorm that you couldn't focus on a productive response, but you can't admit to that. By retreating and then going back to him later, you give yourself a chance to collect your thoughts, reevaluate your plan, and take him by surprise.

Be careful, though. You can't wade into Round 2 with any old arguments and expect to win. You have to use the most powerful arguments at your command. These are not necessarily the arguments that would thrill you the most but rather those he wants to hear—the ones that meet his personal needs.

OVER AND OVER AGAIN

Paranoid bosses have small minds and short memories. As intelligent and capable as they may be, their propensity to worry about tomorrow is often far stronger than their ability to remember how valuable you were to them yesterday. Remind them over and over again how valuable you are. You might find this tiresome, but when you look at the more successful people, it's obvious that some of them find scratching backs a whole lot easier than having to work for a living.

8

You're the One

Good for you. You've learned how to identify and meet the needs of others. That'll help, but meeting needs marginally will probably not be enough. Plan on meeting them with overkill. Make your bosses and others believe that reaching their goals without you would be difficult, if not impossible. They must feel that they wouldn't want to risk angering you, much less losing you. This may sound like something out of a country and western ballad, but it's not; it's an integral part of office politics.

Indispensability is a myth; anyone can be replaced. But that's logic talking. If the people you have to motivate act as if they are indispensable, they aren't being logical, they're being vulnerable, and that's your clue to knowing that you can trip them up and con them into thinking that they can't meet their needs without you.

SOONER, QUICKER, LONGER, LOUDER, ETC.

Tim started with the company as a salesman and eventually worked his way up to executive vice president, all while functioning as product manager for pollution control devices. Tim eventually sold forty million dollars' worth of things. Not once, however, was the line profitable. It constantly drained the corporate coffers. Every year the CEO gave Tim a budget for advertising, sales meetings, and travel expenses. And every year the competition creamed him.

This company was founded—and almost wholly owned by—Ben, who made ten large fortunes on its automation products. Ben was totally self-centered. When he wasn't thinking of himself, he focused only on the person who looked back at him in a mirror.

Tim knew this. He spent most of his time being a one-man cheering section, booster club, and PR flack for Ben. Others tried to do the same, and some of them found their own ways to motivate Ben, but none as outlandishly as Tim.

When someone argued with Ben at a staff meeting, Tim led the defensive counterattack. Tim's sales presentations were often nothing more than a recitation of the company's past successes, all attributed to Ben's wisdom. Tim once stooped so low as to put together a chorus of singers from the accounting department. That in itself wasn't so bad, but when they sang "Nobody's as good as us" to the tune of "Merrily We Roll Along," everyone moaned. Everyone except Ben and Tim, that is. Ben beamed, and Tim gloated.

I guess that when you run a company that pays you millions, you can always tolerate a particular product line's losing a few hundred thousand dollars a year. That's obviously the way Ben felt. Tim was an expert at supplying the adulation that Ben craved, and Ben was willing to pay handsomely for it.

Many people saw Tim as nothing more than a shallow individual whose main talent was positioning his nose so it could give Ben a thorough prostate exam. I used to feel that way. Instead of competing with Tim and making his accomplishments look small in comparison to my own, I allowed my ego to direct my actions. Ben wanted praise, and Tim gave it to him. I, on the other hand, gave him nothing but arguments and petulance when we disagreed. He responded by making Tim rich while making me look for another job. Tim knew what was going on, but I sure didn't, and I don't believe Ben had any idea how much he was being manipulated.

There's nothing unique or new about this story. Tim didn't invent politics. It was widely used long before he or I arrived on the scene. Lots of people use the techniques described on these pages. Unless they want something from you, not one of those people is busy working to meet your goals. They have their own goals to worry about.

Split your pursuit of satisfaction into two parts. One part we have already discussed: providing the right motivation to the right people. The second part is getting the most for your efforts. Resources are never unlimited. At any point in time, there is only so much money for raises and bonuses, so many promotions, and so many favors to go around. The less everybody else gets, the more is available to you. Conversely, the more they get, the less you can have. Without a fight, you can't possess what others already have.

Every work environment is competitive. You may compete only with a boss's image of perfection, but you are probably also working with others who want the same things you want. To fight them off, you have no choice but to motivate sooner, quicker, longer, louder, and more extravagantly than they do.

It's natural to look at your competition as enemies you must defeat to prevent them from taking what you would rather have for yourself. Following this view of life, however, you may focus on making someone else lose when you should be working only to make yourself win.

As my friend Al Hazzard can tell you, winning is not necessarily the same as forcing someone else to lose. Upon hearing through the company grapevine that he and Larry were the leading candidates for a new high-level job, Al went to his boss to find out what was going on. When the boss confirmed the rumor, Al said that he wanted the job. But then he took a wrong turn and gave an extended dissertation on Larry's weaknesses. Larry did pretty much the same in bad-mouthing Al. Acting more like gamecocks or pit bulls than like managers, the two of them spent the next few weeks going out of their way to put each other down. Unwilling to promote a person whose behavior was childish and unproductive, however, the boss gave the job to someone else.

By saying nasty things about Larry, Al thought he was helping his own cause, but that was not the case. He succeeded only in coming across as childish. Larry looked no better. The boss wondered, "Will these idiots be able to work together?" Unable to answer the question, he couldn't give the job to either one.

Don't do what they did. Instead of bringing up a competitor's faults, emphasize your strengths in areas where the other guy is weak. Be forceful and passionate in making your case, but level a direct attack on people only if you are acting in self-defense or if you must disable them before they disable you. We'll deal with those situations in chapter 14.

A NECESSARY EVIL

No matter what the boss thinks of you personally, he'll want to keep you around if he perceives you as a necessary evil. To boost your image in this regard:

Help bosses focus on what they like to do. Many bosses will do something only if it gives them high visibility and makes them look good. Others focus on fun or ego-fulfilling activities. The boss who views himself as a world-class designer will go to any extreme to avoid delegating work in that area, particularly to anyone who might be better than he is.

Become the boss's hatchet man. A "hatchet man" does another person's dirty work. Confronting an opponent would force the boss to venture out from his bunker and expose himself to harm, so the hatchet man stands in for him. Specific duties include: explaining unpopular company policies to irate employees, firing people, and publicly claiming responsibility for dumb or particularly repugnant ideas that are really the boss's.

On a more mundane basis, your boss may not be that egotistical. He could merely be uncomfortable when making public appearances or being a company spokesperson. If that's the case, he'd be thrilled to have you do those things for him.

Do what others can't do. Some things must be done, but if no one knows how, take advantage of the opportunity and take care of it yourself. If your boss can't download a file from the corporate E-mail system, do it for him.

If you don't have a unique skill, develop one. Become so adept at it that the boss and everyone else in the company looks to you whenever that need arises. The more frequently that happens, the more often you can show how important you are. Pick something necessary. Not blacksmithing. That won't be important in most companies. But, you can be the tax expert, the government regulations expert, the point of contact with local newspapers, or the engineer most familiar with a certain design. If those ideas don't fit, then how about being the in-house computer whiz or the company's ecology specialist.

You can be a resource in areas unconnected to your job. How about your boss's job? Could you solve a problem for him that doesn't fall into your area of responsibilities? Even if he hasn't asked, do it. If you don't, someone else will.

Do you have personal knowledge of a remote city where an important new customer is located? Maybe you can be the Internet access adviser. How about languages? Can you translate, interpret, write, or read any of them better than your co-workers? How about computer languages? Think hard and volunteer your services the instant you come up with something.

Do what everyone else hates to do. In addition to observing what your bosses want and like, pay attention to those activities they detest. Bosses are beset by pressures that promise no rewards, yet cannot be ignored. Somebody has to grind out monthly reports to top management or the board of directors, attend staff meetings, and fly out to visit those angry customers.

Your boss can do all these things, and perhaps he usually does, but maybe he has other priorities this week. Maybe he says so, and maybe you're smart enough to detect his angst and capitalize on it. Do a good job and he'll appreciate your help. Who knows? He might even ask for your help again, and then start relying on you. If you can get him that far, he'll be right where you want him.

9

Networking

Doing a job while getting satisfaction from it is hard work—a lot of hard work. Don't do it all by yourself. Figure out a way to motivate others to do some of it for you. The same applies to every other aspect of meeting corporate goals, your boss's personal goals, or your own goals. Do the things you can do best, while motivating others to perform any tasks you find distasteful, don't understand, or can't do as well or as quickly as they can.

Let's start understanding these others by giving them a collective name: your support network. Such a network consists of those people with whom you can establish a mutually beneficial political relationship. Networks typically consist of peers, subordinates, relatives, friends from outside of work, business contacts, and even bosses. How does this cast of characters get on your network? You put them there. Some of them may be dear to you, and others you may detest, but all have the potential to scratch your back if you first scratch theirs. We've already talked about your bosses, so let's examine some of the other residents on your network.

SUBORDINATES

People who report to you can make your life either easy or awful. The choice is yours. Do you try to show 'em who's the boss? If that's what you want, I hope you succeed. If what you really want is greater productivity, a raise, or a promotion, however, imperiousness may not be the best way to get it.

Tyrants use pressure tactics to get their way, but barking out orders has limited effectiveness. Once subordinates discover that you have nothing else to offer but brute force, they will play politics with you, hide from you, and circumvent your power whenever they can. Grudgingly doing as little work as possible, they'll blame scapegoats and bombard you with all sorts of other excuses just to cover up for their unwillingness to do more. Once they discover that you treat them well only when they say what you want to hear, they may rarely tell you the truth—at least, not all of it.

I can almost hear you protesting that you wouldn't be so foolish. Perhaps not, but I've seen a boatload of blowhards go over the same precipice before you. If your thinking is ego-driven, not only will you fall for political chicanery, you'll fall hard.

Irate at a lack of response to his bullying, the despotic boss believes that he can meet the needs of his subordinates in only two ways: by hiring them, and by being generous enough not to fire them. He is otherwise unconcerned with their needs, responding to them only with pressure and terror tactics. To fully motivate subordinates, he should focus on his goals and change his tactics if necessary, but that would be too logical. Running on pure ego, many bosses focus only on flexing their political muscle.

But you don't have to be brain-dead. Do things the easy

way. Focus on your goals, and use subordinates to help you meet those goals. Delegate tasks to them so you can liberate more of your own time. Instead of wasting that time on work that benefits only the company's stockholders or your boss, use it for your own political gain.

Subordinates don't have to know your goals, but they must know precisely what you expect from them in each assignment. Set standards as high as you like, but make sure they know exactly what you want, and when you want it. Define any progress reports you want, and specify whether you want them written or oral. When you have finished defining an assignment, ask the person to repeat his or her understanding of what it is, and don't blow your stack if you have to clarify a few points. To avoid confusion later on, ask the subordinate to document the assignment in writing, and don't hesitate to make written corrections to that document as you see fit.

In reviewing subordinates, presume in advance that they will never work just to meet your goals. Ask what *their* goals are, and strive to accommodate them. Tell them that if they produce for you by doing what you ask, you will try as hard as possible to see that their goals are met. Just don't make promises you know you can't keep. Some of their goals may be monetary, but others may be associated with the type of work they do, their hours, the way their offices are furnished, the extent to which they can telecommute, and the authority they'll have. Even if you don't have the last word on all matters, if you broadly discuss your subordinates' needs, you will increases your chances of being able to meet as many of them as possible.

At the earliest opportunity, give each subordinate a free "gift." Scratch first. You could compliment them, share credit for an accomplishment, or permit them to look good to top management. Money is not required. The point is to offer people the hope that they can fulfill at least some of their goals, and to treat them with dignity. Everybody wants that.

Consider each person as an individual. Does she produce what you have asked her to produce? If she does, extend another favor, and then another. If you catch her going over your head, trying to outshine you, or throwing nothing but attitude and excuses your way, take her aside and tell her bluntly that her behavior is unacceptable. Tell her where she has gone wrong and give her tips on how to improve her performance.

As you might imagine, this approach to management cannot succeed unless you have people who are at the top of both the talent pool and the integrity pool. It will also fail if you treat your troops as incompetent idiots who need you to look over their shoulders every few seconds, or if you bog them down with stupid, time-wasting meetings.*

A shortsighted, fear-driven boss hires only those people who are "safe" and "cheap." They'll get the job done with the right supervision, they do not command top dollar, and they are not ambitious enough or talented enough to threaten their bosses. This is theory. In practice, you may spend so much time supervising inept subordinates and correcting their mistakes that you'll have no time left for motivating your boss. That would be monumentally dumb, so don't do it.

No one is competent enough to be the perfect subordinate, innocent enough to work for substandard wages, and desperate enough to accept being treated like garbage. Ignoring this truth, many employers waste a fortune by continuously recruiting, training, chewing up, and replacing people who accept low salaries. These, of course, are the same bosses who will look at you with a straight face and insult your intelligence by telling you that they can never find good people. Of

*Is there any other kind of meeting?

course there are no good people who are willing to work for long hours at substandard wages and be treated like garbage, but some bosses never give up trying to prove otherwise.

Wake up to reality before you fall into the same trap. Ditch any extra ego you are carrying around. Hire only the best people you can find, afford, and satisfy. Tell them precisely what you want, treat them with respect, and step aside so they can do the company's work while you spend the bulk of your own time meeting your personal goals.

PEERS

You can also delegate assignments to people whose rank is more or less the same as yours, but only if they don't realize that you are manipulating them. No matter how friendly you are with your peers, don't ever forget that they are competing with you for whatever raises and promotions are available. They may not be competitors in *your* mind, but no matter how much they smile and act civilized, some of them will see you only as an enemy. When things get tight, they may unhesitatingly cut your political throat.

Be civil and pleasant to everyone, but be discreet and selective about which peers to motivate. Take a guess. Whose favors might you really need some day? Who is most likely to be promoted to a position from which he or she could be greatly valuable to you?

As soon as you decide whose help you are most likely to need, put them in your debt by using all the observational, back-scratching, schmoozing, listening, and stroking techniques described in earlier chapters. Do something they will appreciate. Suggest that you meet for lunch (one at a time, of

course) to discuss ways in which you might be mutually beneficial to each other. Identify problems you can help them
solve, and offer to do so with no strings attached. Pick up the
tab for lunch.

These strategies may not work if you need something
immediately. They are investments that must be nurtured by
an ongoing relationship in which you continue to schmooze
and be helpful. None of this requires you to invest much time
or effort. Maybe you can alert your intended target to some
inside information affecting her job. If not, perhaps you can
just make yourself available to commiserate if she seems upset
about anything. Be on the lookout for motivational opportunities and capitalize on them.

If an emergency arises and the person you need is not
already in your debt, put him or her there not only with
lunch, but by schmoozing, stroking, and openly offering to
scratch first if the other person will scratch you back in a certain way. The more attractive your offer, the more likely it
will be to succeed.

OTHERS AT THE SAME LEVEL AS YOUR SUBORDINATES

If anyone can find that old paperwork you're looking for, it's
Mary, the assistant to the sales vice president. Mary's not an
uncooperative person, but although she is below you in the
hierarchy, she is not in your chain of command. You can't tell
her what to do. To make things worse, she is swamped doing
work for her boss.

Mary's job is to support that boss, not the employee popu-
lation at large. How can you get her to take the time to do
something for you? You can't make demands on her and then

complain to her boss if she declines to help. She would tell him she was too busy seeing to his priorities to worry about yours, and she would be right.

The only way to get Mary on your side is to motivate her. You have always scratched her back by being nice to her. You say hello, you smile when you meet, you ask how she is doing in graduate school and how her brother is feeling after his skiing accident. You always act as if you are concerned if she tells you about her personal problems.

What do you do, now that you need her? One possibility is to use oldest, most ingenious motivational tactic in the annals of business—the request for assistance. Don't demand her help. Instead, ask for it and explain why it is important. She may pitch in because she can see that it's essential or because you're a nice person who has asked in a nice way. But if she is still resistant, augment your offer. Several ways come to mind:

- Promise to run interference for her if her boss fears that he will suffer because she has neglected his work for yours.
- Get her boss to ask her to help you. Motivate him to issue the orders to her. If he doesn't owe you a favor, perhaps you can "scratch his back." What could you offer him?
- Mary has other responsibilities, so don't be surprised if she rebels at the prospect of doubling her workload just to make you happy. Perhaps you can help her find the time for your stuff if you do some of her other work. Could you answer her phones for an hour or so? Complete that important proposal she has been working on?

Pardon my being a cynic, but everybody has a price. Don't limit your thinking. Maybe Mary would like her desk chair fixed. How do you know what her price is? If you don't know and can't figure it our by trial and error, ask her, and then decide whether you are willing to pay. Maybe you can offer her a trade. You will do "x" for her if she does "y" for you. You'd be in trouble trading with subordinates every time you wanted them to do something, but you have nothing to lose by trying to trade with Mary.

BOSSES OTHER THAN YOUR OWN

Your best bet with this crowd is to treat them as you treat your own boss. Be careful, however. If you appear too aggressive in making a reputation for yourself in top management circles, your own boss may feel threatened. You can't be too laid back, either. You have to maintain visibility in case management concludes that your boss or any of his peers has to be replaced.

This sounds like walking a tightrope, and it is, but you can handle it. Be as much of a hero as you like to other bosses. Just don't steal glory from your own boss. Make sure you do nothing that makes him looks bad in comparison to you. If he is in the room when you are paid a compliment, talk "we" instead of "I" and publicly share the stage with him. At the very least, credit him with fully supporting you.

SUPPLIERS AND CUSTOMERS

Those who do business with a company may know more about its ins and outs than those who work there. If the place where you work is not paying its bills, changing its purchasing habits, or running surprisingly slow on deliveries, vendors

and buyers will know something is happening. They may not
know exactly what that is, but their feelings may be more
deeply rooted in fact than your own in-house rumor mill.

Someone doing business with your company probably
works with other companies in similar businesses. Maybe
they are aware of some boss who is desperately trying to fill
a job you'd love to have. An advertising manager friend of
mine was going nowhere in his job search some years ago
until he tapped into his network of salespeople who had been
selling him ad space in magazines. They told him about a
couple of places that were looking for just the expertise he
was offering.

Suppliers and customers are relatively easy to befriend. As
long as you don't want them to buy anything, customers can
be plied with news of bargains or product availability. Suppliers want orders or information that can lead to orders. All
these people will be most willing to trade favors with you.

COMPETITORS, OTHER EMPLOYERS, AND INDUSTRY WATCHERS

Join industry associations to whatever extent you can spare
the time, and go to meetings, but don't just sit there. Make a
name for yourself by running for office, writing articles in
their professional magazine, or both. Get to know the people.
Let them get to know you. You probably won't learn much
confidential information (and you certainly shouldn't divulge
any, either), but you may find news about job openings, or
information you can use as motivational fodder for your
boss. Make a good enough impression and maybe someone
will try to hire you away from your current workers' paradise.

You say this is impossible in your situation? Perhaps you

can still read applicable trade journals and keep up to date on who is doing what. Maybe you will see an interesting article on a situation you can capitalize on.

Look in particular for authors who have enough clout to give your career a boost. Call one who is not with a competitive company. Put him on your network, and be prepared to motivate him. If he senses that you have nothing to offer him in return for his time, he may not want anything to do with you. Tell him you and he are interested in the same topics and that you liked his article. Schmooze with him. Maybe he would be interested in writing an article with you. If you prefer, write first to introduce yourself, and then call.

FRIENDS AND RELATIVES

Close friends and relatives can probably be trusted more than co-workers. But the qualities that make someone a friend do not necessarily render that person an expert in job satisfaction and how to get it. Aunt Sue may be the sweetest person in the world and a genius at tax accounting, but that doesn't mean she knows anything about computer science or how to handle a boss like yours. Maybe she does, but before you take her advice as gospel, ask her where she got her ideas and whether she ever personally put them to use.

Lynn across the street is your best friend, and she has volunteered to help you get a job by arranging an appointment with her uncle, who owns a company in town. That's terrific, but is he in a business you know anything about? Does he have any job openings you could fill? You may not be able to avoid this uncle without offending Lynn, but you should not meet him with unrealistic expectations. If you are busy in what seem to be more fruitful directions, you can call the uncle and explain that you thought he might want to first chat over the phone rather than waste his time on matters that might not amount to anything.

A MATTER OF NEED

The purpose of networking extends far beyond expanding your social circles on a grand scale. Please remember that, and don't write people off just because they are beneath you in the hierarchical scheme of things or because they have nothing to offer you today. You never know who will be promoted tomorrow or who will marry the boss's son or daughter. Neither do you know what you might want from them tomorrow.

Don't expect anyone to cooperate solely on the strength of your being a nice person. Conversely, don't depend on them to fold and capitulate just because you fume and belch forth venomous threats. Instead of thinking of you as a friend or as a threat to their security, people will be more dependable if you can get them to think of you as a necessity.

10

Communications

Saedid nasthg uoh tgnigna hcxefosse cor pehtsign itacinum moc.

The sentence above is *not* a misprint. It has been published here exactly as I wrote it, and it *does* make sense. Can't you read it? Why not? Are you illiterate or just dense?

Only kidding. If you can't understand that sentence, the reason is that you are reading the letters from left to right. But I didn't write them in that direction. I can't imagine why you didn't know that. To comprehend my meaning more readily, you have to reverse the sequence of the letters:

Com municati ngisthep roc essofexch
angingt hou ghtsan dideas.

Still confused? Change the points at which the letter groups are separated:

Communicating is the process of
exchanging thoughts and ideas.

These are the same letters we started with, but the meaning has changed considerably. Surely you can see from this little demonstration that communicating is a lot more complicated than heaving a bucket of alphabet soup in the air and letting the pieces fall wherever they may. It's also more complicated than saying or writing the first thing that comes to your mind.

GET THEIR ATTENTION

The best argument will accomplish nothing if no one hears it or reads it. Do people stop what they're doing just to listen you when you speak or read when they receive a memo from you? No. They may hear the sounds you make in talking, and they may see which parts of the alphabet you use as you write, but their minds may be on altogether different topics. You have to motivate them to pay attention. You do this by giving them reason to believe they will benefit by doing so.

Speak up when you want to talk to someone. Shout as loud as you must to be heard over everyone else. Speak as directly and as forcefully as you can and bring up a topic that you know will command immediate attention. You could say:

> *I'd like to talk to you as soon as possible about a potential problem in our Tokyo office.*

but that's much too long–winded. By the time you get to the word "problem," someone else may shout you down. Get rid of the introductory stuff and try a more direct approach:

> *We have a potential problem in our Tokyo office.*

This is an improvement, but it may also be too weak to get

the attention you need. What *is* the problem? Maybe it's the
new wallpaper they want. Is it out of stock? Will they have to
select a new pattern? Or is the problem of a more pressing
nature? Spell it out.

> *Our Tokyo office will lose its biggest*
> *customer if we don't act fast.*

That's better. You have said just enough to attract interest,
but not so much that your explanation can be avoided. To the
contrary, you may have everyone within earshot holding their
breath to hear the details of your Tokyo story.

The same approach applies in writing. People will eventually read your memos and reports, but if you want your stuff
read first, give it an attention-getting subject. In a letter about
budgets, for example, do you say that the subject is "budgets"
or "anticipated cost overruns"? The latter, of course, is much
more likely to generate interest.

Be careful. If you cry wolf too often, you will soon be seen
as an alarmist whose fears are exaggerated. You can avoid
this fate by catching yourself before representing a problem as
the catastrophe of the century. Another hazard of getting
attention is bringing up a problem without saying what its
solution should be. As the bearer of bad news, you may be
treated as if you caused the problem rather than having
merely reported it.

You should have a solution in mind before you announce a
problem. You may even want to state that you have both:

> *I know how we can prevent the Tokyo office*
> *from losing its biggest customer.*

That will get the attention you want. Now you can state the
problem and use one-thing-leads-to-another logic to explain

its ramifications. Having said that you have solutions, state them, but not until your thinking is explained step by step. Leaving the payoff for last insures that your entire argument will register, not just the opening line.

LOCK AND LOAD

Many of your day-to-day job problems are associated with miscommunication. This is because regardless of what you say or how you say it, people will draw conclusions about it. If those conclusions are not the ones you want them to reach, the fault is entirely yours. Not theirs, not mine, but yours.

Even if everybody were looking at the same words on paper, different people will construe them in various ways. Parents see things differently from their children, and corporate bosses have a take on economic news that doesn't begin to resemble that of their employees. All bosses do not feel the same way on issues, and neither do all employees.

You may disagree with someone's point of view, but if you don't know what that point of view is, you are doing nothing more than taking a shot in the dark in trying to communicate with him. How can you tell what he is thinking? You have to identify, consider, and meet his needs. To schmooze with an engineer who is probably a technology freak, talk about microprocessors and the like. If he is a CEO and more likely to be concerned about profits and sales, focus on business. In either case, remember never to say anything that will turn his ego against you.

Ask yourself what fears people may have. Address those fears in your conversations and correspondence with them. If the boss is concerned about costs, don't just tell him of your scheme to take care of the Tokyo problem, tell him how little that scheme will cost him and how certain it is to work.

SPIN

Assume you want to do (or are doing) one thing, but your boss wants you to do something else. Rather than turn her down, give her a choice. Yes, you'll be happy to move in the direction she is advocating, but if you did, some other project would suffer. Lay out the facts for her, emphasizing only those that support your preference.

Downplay potentially conflicting information she may have mentioned. Tell her that it's meaningless, trivial, unconfirmed, or mistaken. If she hasn't brought it up, don't volunteer it. Highlight penalties to be paid if you go in any direction but the one you favor. Disregard or minimize the impact of everything else.

Focus on her needs and her objectives. Does she enjoy the limelight? If so, show her how one alternative will result in her ability to achieve the greatest glory. You may actually prefer that alternative because it gets the company to pay your way to the south of France for a week, but keep that reason to yourself. Tell everyone how you hate to travel.

There's a name for the twisting of the facts to suit a particular purpose: spin. Typical uses for spin are:

- making bad news sound like good news.
- highlighting some facts and burying others.
- shifting the blame by offering scapegoats.
- revealing "new" facts or mitigating circumstances that help to solve a problem.

- using a new view of known facts to explain the previously unexplainable.
- finding a silver lining in what most rational people would see as utter disaster.

Spin takes "emphasizing the positive" to extremes, and often for selfish purposes. The art of the so-called "spin doctor" is to know how to take facts and explanations right up to the edge of truthfulness and believability, without falling over into a bottomless pit of lies.

I never cease to be amazed at the gall of some executives. They will tell you something like "*We* had a good year, and *our* profits reached record highs." In their next breath, however, they'll say they can't afford to give you a raise. When "we" are making money and you can't get a share of it, you are clearly not one of the people they had in mind when they mentioned "our" profits.

They don't see how blatantly offensive their duplicity is. Nor do they realize that once you discover how one-sided their spin is, you will quickly lose interest in whether "we" show profits next year. I hope you are not so shortsighted with your own subordinates.

Many bosses are not visionaries. As a class, they tend to think only of today and only of themselves. When you communicate with them, you must:

- highlight what they want to hear.
- suppress or explain away problems, which they do not want to hear about.
- suggest numerous scapegoats for them to cast blame on.
- give them most of the credit for the good news.
- take the rest of the credit for yourself.

Disgusting, isn't it? You want just to do your job, and you

get caught up in all this spin nonsense. A engineering manager friend of mine in Silicon Valley put it best in describing his work: "Much of what I do has nothing to do with computers, it's about making my boss look good and keeping my job."

LEAVE THEM NO OPTIONS

Never point out to your boss that you are helping him make a fool of that other boss who is competing with him for that big job at headquarters. You also should not tell him that without you, he could never impress his boss. Even if they are true, such statements are self-serving and likely to be considered presumptuous, offensive, or both.

You can, however, say that you have done something, that it was better than someone else's efforts, and that a boss named Harrison liked what you did.

> I completed the report you requested and presented it in your absence to Bill Harrison at his staff meeting yesterday. I had the report and the slides printed in full color rather than in black and white. The presentation from accounting, by comparison, had chart after chart of numbers and words that in many instances were too small to read. Bill thanked me and said that he was impressed.

Note that the example does *not* document how much more it cost to have everything printed in color, and how many hours it took you to make the graphs come out looking perfect. Your boss probably doesn't care how hard you worked or, within reason, how much you spent. If the results you get are the results he wants, you win.

Give information to people in such a way that they have no

choice but to come to the conclusions you want them to reach. You do that by telling them only those facts you want them to know, and then by using spin to let them come to conclusions on their own. Of course you can summarize and state your conclusions, but your conclusions don't matter unless you can motivate others to reach them. If you give the right spin to the right facts, your readers will have no choice but to come to those conclusions on their own.

Look again at the sample paragraph shown above. As written, it represents a potential problem. If your boss were paranoid enough, he might be rather angry at you after reading such a memo. Even though Bill Harrison was impressed, *you* got the credit. Your boss may prefer keeping at least some of that credit, so let's tack on one additional sentence.

> I completed the report you requested and presented it in your absence to Bill Harrison at his staff meeting yesterday. I had the report and the slides printed in full color rather than in black and white. The presentation from accounting, by comparison, had chart after chart of numbers and words that in many instances were too small to read. Bill thanked me and said that he was impressed. I told him that what we did was based entirely on your instructions.

Given only the information that he sees in this paragraph, the boss would have to conclude that you did exactly what he would have wanted you to do.

Of course, not every situation is that simple. Maybe the best news of the day is that you believe you have finally overcome a problem the boss is worried about:

> At that point I tried the JR-3 combination and it worked! For the first time, everything performed right up to its design limits. We will run the machine again tomorrow to confirm our results.

Do you see mention of problems that might crop up tomorrow? Not here. Nor do you see any indication that the observed good results were flukes. If the writer has any concerns or reservations about what might happen tomorrow, she kept them to herself. To her boss, she reported only that she accomplished something, and that she anticipates more of the same the next day. Best of all, nothing she said can be taken to threaten her boss.

If you are worried about the next day, don't just spout out bad news. Bring forth a scapegoat.

> The weather was dry and sunny; ideal for our survey. Rain is predicted tomorrow, however, so we may not be able to attract as much of a crowd as we got today.

But don't stop there. Show why you will get the job done, scapegoat or not.

> The weather was dry and sunny; ideal for our survey. Rain is predicted tomorrow, however, so we may not be able to attract as much of a crowd as we got today if we stay in the same place on the approach road. So, if the weather is poor, we will move to the mall and theater entrance areas. You can tell headquarters that the job will get done no matter how bad the weather is.

WINNING ARGUMENTS

When we want to win an argument, we too often attempt to force our adversary to lose. This is often quite counterproductive, since some people may do anything to avoid losing an argument.

If what you want is to convince someone to come around to a point of view, you may have to take pains to not state it as your own. If the person you have to convince is an arrogant boor who cannot stomach losing an argument to you, presenting your actual opinion may create or prolong a fight. State your view merely as one option, but do not tell him that it's your view, and spin the facts so only one conclusion can be drawn from them.

Chris Johns is a master at winning arguments. When his purposes are suited, Chris often appears to take a position diametrically opposed to his real position. He noticed that certain people would fight him no matter what he wanted. He simply took advantage of that. If they wanted to be negative, he reasoned, let them be negative.

The first time I saw him do this, we were in a meeting that was called to decide whether to locate the company's California office in Los Angeles or in San Francisco. Chris preferred the latter because his son was in school at Berkeley, but Tom Greene, the company controller, wanted desperately to look good to the boss, and he didn't mind if Chris looked bad in the process.

Just before he began to talk, Chris slipped me a note asking me just to watch but say nothing. He then got up and gave an impassioned plea for the office to be in Los Angeles. *Los Angeles?* What was he doing?

I thought Chris's cost figures seemed high, but it took me a few minutes to see that they were high on purpose. When Tom rose to speak, he destroyed the economics of Chris's proposal and suggested that the office be in San Francisco. Chris gracefully praised Tom's research and changed his vote. Tom was the hero on that occasion, but the office was opened right where Chris wanted it—in San Francisco.

Didn't Chris look foolish to his boss for suggesting an expensive alternative? Perhaps, but only temporarily. He scapegoated an L.A. real estate broker. In any event, Chris's focus was not on always impressing the boss at all times and at all costs. In this particular exchange, his focus was on being able to conveniently visit his son during business trips. He had nothing to gain by divulging that, however, so he didn't. He said what he had to say to get that office where he wanted it. This deception isn't always workable, but just like Chris, every once in a blue moon you may be able to reach a goal by making others believe that they have won an argument with you.

DON'T MAKE IT PERSONAL

One final tip on spin and on winning arguments: differences of opinion can never be resolved by making them personal. If you force someone to defend his honor, his intelligence, or his integrity, you transform job situations into personal vendettas that can continue long after business matters have been resolved.

This is why insults or slurs never help. Words like *stupid, moronic, incompetent,* or *awful* are inflammatory. So what if they're accurate? They don't change anything, and they can stiffen someone's resistance to you. If you don't like what people have said or done, you won't like it any more after insulting them. A more effective approach is to ask (not demand) that they explain further.

"Yes, but if we did that, how could we avoid…"

or

"Doesn't that lead to a problem with the…"

Similarly, "Shouldn't that number be...?" is much better than "This is wrong." For that matter, "Have you noticed the time?" is an improvement on "You're late."

MODALITIES

Communicating face-to-face is best in four situations:

1. For schmoozing.
2. When you are in the same room as the person with whom you wish to communicate, and you have no need to hide anything from others in that room.
3. When you want to be extremely forceful in making an impression or an argument. You probably can't motivate someone to hire you, for example, if she knows nothing about you except what she sees on paper.
4. When you want to motivate someone who is most comfortable interfacing with a living, breathing human being.

If you can't meet with a person eyeball to eyeball, the telephone is the preferred alternative. Using the phone saves travel time, but all it gives you are words and tone of voice. You get neither personal contact nor the time to plan and rethink your choice of words. You can, however, schmooze quite effectively on the phone.

You can't schmooze at all in writing, but it does offer you several advantages:

1. You don't have to communicate "off the top of your head." You can plan your message before sending it; often before the recipient knows it is coming.

2. If you say something stupid, you can take it back and no one will ever know that you said it in the first place. You can than write and rewrite until you say precisely what you want to say.

3. Writing lets someone receive your message even if he or she is unavailable when you wrote it. You don't have to force it on them. They can read it at a time of their convenience, when they may be more receptive to your position.

4. It offers you a buffer behind which you can state your views without interruption and without being bullied by dirty looks or other pressures.

5. It documents what you did or did not say. Put something on paper and no one can get away with accusing you of not saying it or of saying something else.

You can also use facsimile or fax messages, which became commonplace in the 1980s, and E-mail, which many people are using in the 1990s. Both offer all the advantages of written communication, combined with the speed of the telephone. And, they are both ideal for dealing with those people with whom you must communicate, but who never shut up when engaged in conversation.

Your ability to motivate or to take charge of matters may depend on which communication methods you use. For example, if you are traveling and you want to avoid a broad-scale interrogation when you report in, send in a fax. Turn off your cellular phone for the evening, don't look at your E-mail until tomorrow morning, and be on your way.

How you communicate can determine whether you succeed at motivating a stranger—perhaps a prospective employer—to meet you. If you were to visit or call that person when he or she was busy, you might not get an audience, and your story would probably be rushed. If you first send a letter of introduction, on the other hand, the person would have already received your complete sales pitch and might be more willing to see you.

PRECISION

Ideas you wish to communicate must be complete and unambiguous. If they aren't, you will have only yourself to blame for the resultant misery that falls on your head and knocks you down.

For example, you'd probably laugh at me if I told you that two plus two equals six. And yet it does. I know you've been taught that "two plus two equals four," but that is true only if we are talking about two identical items added to two more of the same. If two things are added to two different things, the total can be anything but four. For example, *two* quarters plus *two* nickels adds up to the same amount of money as *six* dimes. As I said, two plus two equals six.

Assume that your boss called this morning to ask when you would finish that assignment he gave you yesterday. Anxious to make a good impression and just about done with the work, you tell him that he will have your report "after lunch." Happy with your progress, he goes on to something else, and you return to your solitude, unaware that you have just gotten yourself into trouble.

Your problem is that this man is absolutely anal when it comes to time. To him, "after lunch" means "as soon as I return to my office after eating my tuna sandwich at about 12:30 P.M." Once you told him "after lunch," he rearranged his afternoon so he could review your work between 1 and 2, and then meet with his boss.

You don't show up when he expects you, so at 12:35 he starts working on a project he hadn't planned on addressing until later in the week. He doesn't have the time to finish that project, however, and tomorrow his schedule is completely jammed up. Tonight, he anticipates having to look at your work instead of finishing some reading he was doing at home. By the time he finishes meeting with his boss, it's almost 4 P.M., he sees that you still haven't appeared, and he's ready to kill you.

Oblivious to any of this, you go about your business. "After lunch" to *you* means "not before noon, but no later than 5 P.M." Other priorities came up early in the afternoon, but you assumed there would still be plenty of time to finish up before you went home. You put everything else aside at about 3, and you close the door. You complete the boss's report an hour later, and you stride over to his office expecting congratulations on finishing a little earlier than you had promised.

He takes the report, but he doesn't seem at all impressed. Instead of telling you why he is upset, he just sits there and glowers at you (oh, I forgot to tell you; he's a terrible communicator and he hates confrontations). It doesn't matter at that point how good your report was. You'll walk out of that meeting feeling that he is impossible to please, while he gets the impression that you are unreliable. No wonder you don't get along with him.

Whose fault was all this—his? He is partially to blame, but don't focus on that. If life were a matter of looking skyward to a wise arbitrator who would solve all our communication problems, the boss would be penalized here. But life is not like that. If what you say needs translating before others can grasp it, you'll be the one to suffer the consequences. When you want to communicate an idea, it's up to you to express it in a way the other person can understand, not in some code, not in a language he or she don't know, and not so it can be interpreted in more ways than one.

THE SMART WAY TO MAKE PROMISES

What you do to scratch somebody's back is only one part of politics. The other part is how you promise to do it. That's the part that can get you in trouble if you're not careful.

Speaking personally, I am far too literal and inflexible for my own good. If you say "10 A.M.,"my brain fixes on a period starting at 9:59 and ending at 10:01. Allowing for differences between my watch and yours, I won't mind if you show up as late as 10:05, but after that I'm liable to get very upset at you.

A few minutes one way or another may not seem like a lot, and it isn't much all by itself. But when I am trying to cram twelve hours of work into an eight-hour day, a few minutes is murder on my schedule. If I expect to get a proposal from you at noon and you don't show up with it until five hours later, you will *not* be one of my favorite people. But if you initially told me I'd have it by 3 P.M. and instead delivered it on time or earlier, you would be a hero to me. I should not be this way, and my blood pressure would probably be lower if I weren't, but that's the way I am.

Fortunately for you, I'm not your boss. Unfortunately, I am *not* unique in allowing the clock to rule me. Lots of people are punctuality freaks, and we're all crazy. To avoid upsetting us, don't be more specific about time than necessary.

How do you answer when your boss asks when you will

finish a project? Do you say exactly when? Not if you can be vague. Your best answer is to say something like:

> *I expect to have it done by the middle-*
> *to-latter part of the week.*

If that makes him happy, fine. You now have a lot of latitude. If he wants more precision, however, you can always say:

> *I'm shooting for Wednesday afternoon.*

"Wednesday afternoon," of course, is not the same as "after lunch." The afternoon extends from 12:01 to 6 P.M., still leaving you some leeway.

As you may have noticed, wording such as "I expect…" and "I'm shooting for…" is hardly definite. You should state them as goals, not as drop-dead guarantees. You should also try to build in an escape hatch to suggest that your fulfilling your promise depends on matters beyond your control. An escape hatch is a scapegoat named in advance to cover your you-know-what if you need more time. You might say something like, "I should have no trouble with Wednesday as long as the graphics package from marketing comes in on Tuesday." If you don't expect marketing to deliver until Thursday, you're covered.

But what do you do if you are asked flat out to get a job done at a specific time and date? If it's humanly possible, do it and be the hero, that's what you do.

If you can't, one possible response is to say so. But don't just focus on what you can't do. Focus on what you *can* do and when you can do it. People may accept part of a package late, if they are able to get the rest of it early. For an instruction manual I wrote for a client not too long ago, I knew I'd have problems with two of the chapters. Instead of saying I was going to miss the deadline, I delivered the preface and all the other chapters a week early. I was a few days late on the chapters that had me worried, but nobody cared. Two weeks later, they still hadn't read the manual.

In addition to time, you should be careful in making assurances to others about any accomplishment you may be asked to meet. Promise goals that are big enough to be acceptable, but small enough to be reachable without getting yourself into trouble.

Budgetary considerations are important in many work situations. Suppose your boss asks you to oversee a small project near and dear to that thing he calls a heart. He asks for a budget estimate. Your first calculation is three thousand dollars, but then you realize that if you can scrounge up spare parts and motivate several of your peers to help you "off the books," you can do the job for only five hundred.

But why go out on a limb? Tell him you need three thousand. If he thinks that's too much, he'll speak up. Accept any budget he gives you, but if it is below the first figure you gave him, identify your scapegoats up front and in writing. Once you start on the project, motivate and scrounge all you want. Come in at five hundred (or even a thousand) and you'll be the hero of the month.

AN AUDIENCE OF ONE

No one likes to be thought of as a mere number or as part of a crowd. Speak or write to an audience of one person at a time. What does that person want? What does he or she generally like to hear that the individual you spoke with an hour ago doesn't like?

Address people by their first names. Show concern by asking about their health or the health of their family members. Ask how things are going with any problems that you know about in their personal lives.

Your objective in all this is to convince your audience of one to believe that he or she is the only person on earth who matters to you. Don't let your conversations be interrupted by telephone calls or by people walking in on the two of you. Your life may not hang in the balance, but what you have to say is important, and you should give the other person the impression that he is important as well. Why should he listen to you if you don't take him seriously? If what you have to say is *not* important, don't waste time saying it.

SET UP A MEMO MILL

What you do doesn't speak for itself. It can't, it won't, and it never will. Who's going to turn up the volume and hype the great things you have done—Santa Claus? I'm afraid not. You're going to have to do it by yourself.

Routinely send your bosses memos and reports to keep them informed. They're thirsty for information. But don't just dole out information drop by drop; let 'em have it with a fire hose. What should come out of that nozzle—stories about problems you can't solve? Of course not! The accomplishments of your peers? No. Ford doesn't run commercials for General Motors. Let others write their own memos. Use your memo mill to show how much you have accomplished, how difficult your problems have been, and how you solved them.

PLANS AND UPDATES

Plan out what you expect to accomplish on the job over the coming months. Include plenty of milestones, but make no promises you know you can't keep. Show the plan to your boss. Ask him to suggest any other goals you should set to be as productive as he would like. An integral part of the plan should be regular progress reports. Use each of those reports as an opportunity to motivate the boss by showing how well you are meeting his goals.

As time goes on, update the plan to reflect changing conditions, such as your not being to meet program milestones. Should you say that you screwed up? You could, but you might also insert your toes in a meat grinder. Why would you do that? Control the facts, add spin, toss in a scapegoat, and update your plans accordingly. Compare your performance only to updated plans. You can even delay any updating until after you have first analyzed your performance in a progress report. That way you'll always look good.

COMMUNICATION DOS AND DON'TS

- Limit your use of jargon. If you must use technical expressions, define each one the first time you use it. Assume that those with whom you are communicating have not memorized all your terms.
- Get to the point as soon as you can. You'll come across as boorish if you blast in on people without some introductory "hello and how are you" amenities, but keep that stuff to a minimum. Busy people may become annoyed if they suspect that you are wasting their time.

Table VI — SPACE-WASTERS

Space Waster	Shorter is better, stronger	Comments
I would like to congratulate you	Congratulations	Don't say you'd "like" to do something. Do it!
I firmly believe that this will work	This will work	A definite statement is always better than one based on beliefs
I hate to be a pest, but we need you in Chicago	We need you in Chicago	Your hating to be a pest is not important
This is a very hot project	This is a hot project	How much hotter than hot is very hot?
In order to fix the circuit, you first have to remove the cable	To fix the circuit, you first have to remove the cable	"In order" is always unnecessary
You have to understand that this is the way I write	This is the way I write	Your acquiescence is required, not your understanding
Elaine is a woman who is reliable	Elaine is reliable	Few men are named Elaine

- Focus. Discuss only one subject at a time. Finish that subject before you go on to another. Use up one topic per memo or letter, no more. Your reader may have a short attention span. If you want to tell him about a half-dozen additional subjects, write him a half-dozen additional memos.

- Most people don't read every word and punctuation mark; they glance. To get and keep their attention, write paragraphs that are no longer than six to eight lines. The shorter the better, so they can see and capture your meaning.

- So your readers can easier see your most important ideas at a glance, put them on the first or last line of a paragraph, where they stand out against the white space between paragraphs. That way, readers won't be forced to to slog through line after line of introductory material to find your main points.

- Use bulleted lists to make each item in a series easily distinguishable from one another.

- Boldface, underline, or italicize key words to make them stand out, but only two to three times per page. If you overdo highlighting, nothing stands out.

- Say what you have to say clearly, powerfully, and only once. You may have to repeat yourself in oral conversation if someone hasn't heard you, but repetition in writing wastes space, adds nothing new, and looks stupid.

- Write no memo longer than one page. If everything doesn't fit, choose a smaller type size and narrower margins. Ruthlessly eliminate needless words, sentences, and ideas. Look out also for adjectives and other qualifiers that take up space but add nothing to your message.

Of course, you have to explain things, and that requires

words. All things being equal, though, fewer words make a statement more forceful, easier to read at a glance, and therefore better for communicating.

Whatever you do or say, don't forget that people may have other things to do than to listen to you yak on and on without end. Don't be unsociable, but say what you have to say, and then shut up.

"KNOWLEDGE IS POWER"

Francis Bacon said this almost four hundred years ago, and knowledge still *is* power. To control information is to have power. You can control your boss, your peers, and your subordinates to the degree that you can limit them to knowing only what you want them to know.

Make certain that only you can access your files and records. Of course you need a filing system to help you find things, but who needs you if others can find what they want in your filing cabinet? You might even want to store certain papers in your briefcase and put them in your desk or filing cabinet only if you ever leave that job. I'm not suggesting that you steal any documents or hide classified secrets. Nor am I advising you to refuse to show your boss company documents. He has every right to see them any time he so desires.

However, some of your notes may hold the keys to your successes. For example, you might not want management to know about those line-by-line notes you always prepare to develop and upgrade software code. If they had those notes, they might think you could be replaced by some kid whose salary demands would be far below yours. But who says they have to know those notes exist? Not me. Having had several bosses who thought nothing of rifling through a subordinate's office to get information, I learned years ago to limit what they would find.

In the course of schmoozing, be careful about advertising opinions that might be unpopular with management. You have nothing to gain by telling anyone how much you hate the boss, how many résumés you sent out last week, or the details of the interviews you have lined up next week. Such talk may put you in the good graces of the your friends at work, but loose talk about your complaints can be too easily spread and overheard by your enemies. Even if they keep quiet, the people with whom you eat lunch are not going to chip in to fund your next raise. Instead of schmoozing with them, perhaps you'd be better off spending your time slithering into your boss's good graces.

If you should overhear some interesting news that others may not know, don't blurt it out. Ask yourself what you would have to gain or lose by blabbing it all over the office. Your co-workers may appreciate the information, but will you be helped or hurt if your subordinates or peers know as much as you do? You might be better off first giving that information to the boss, and then parceling it out to others as back-scratching bait. Popularity or power? It's your choice, your focus.

.............11.............

Control Your Time

After focusing, observing, schmoozing, listening, talking, writing, and capitalizing on opportunities, you may feel as if you don't have time for breathing, much less doing your job or having a life outside of work. The truth, however, is that you probably have a lot more free time than you think you have.

IT'S PRICELESS

You intended to update your résumé Tuesday night, but you never got to it. You spent the evening working on a sales proposal your boss wants by 3 P.M. on Wednesday. He sprang it on you with less than a day's notice. Now it's nine in the morning on Wednesday and you're still not done, but you *are* making progress.

Then the phone rings. It's your good friend Gene, who runs the company's San Diego office. He wants to know the telephone number of that trade association guy the two of you met in Washington last December. You give him the number. But then he asks how your mother is, you ask about his kids, and he starts talking about the sorry state of public schools in his area. By the time he hangs up, 9:30 has come and gone.

Just as you focus on that 3 P.M. deadline again, the boss calls you to an emergency meeting. One of your suppliers went on strike, and that affects shipments to virtually every customer. You don't get back to your office until nearly 11. By that time, four people are waiting for you to call them back. Before you know it, noon is just a couple of minutes away, and you still have five hours of work plus one hour of lunch to cram into the remaining three hours before the boss wants that proposal.

You may not know anyone named Gene in San Diego, and you may not have a 3 P.M. deadline to meet, but you probably know what I'm talking about anyway. There are never enough hours in the day to get your job done, so where are you going to find the time to motivate your boss? I'll tell you where. You'll find it by managing your time instead of letting it manage you.

The first thing to learn about time management is that you have no control over time itself. You can't stop it or slow it down any more than you can make it or stretch it. Treat every moment as precious. Once it has passed, you will never get a second chance at it. You will find that making the most of each moment is infinitely more helpful than complaining about the fleeting nature of that moment after it is gone.

PRIORITIES

A priority is a rank-ordering of what is important at any given instant. Priorities are fluid; a list of them is not a straitjacket, it's a time-management tool to hone as you need and to use as you like. If circumstances change, your priorities change, their rankings change, or both. Your top priority is the most important thing you have to do at one instant, but something else may come along that is even more important. Unless and until that happens, however, everything else is secondary.

Paying attention to priorities makes certain that you use your resources according to your needs. Prioritizing serves three important functions.

- It forces you to focus on the activities most important to you.
- It helps you avoid responding only to the person who yells the loudest, instead of the one who represents the most urgent need.
- It minimizes the number of unforeseen crises you will encounter.

What most people do at work depends on the assignments they are given, how frequently their telephone rings, the number and length of the meetings they are asked to attend, and the quantity and complexity of the problems brought to their attention. They spend all their time *reacting* to the demands of others, and no time *acting* to meet their own needs. No wonder they find themselves short on job satisfaction.

You can't stop people from calling you, asking you to sit in on meetings, or coming to you with problems. I know that. And you certainly can't stop your boss from asking you to do things.

I know that, too. You can and you must, however, refuse to permit these factors to interfere with your plans.

What happens when you get a call from a close friend? Do you schmooze regardless of your priorities, or do you excuse yourself, say you'll have to call back, hang up, and get back to work? Unless talking with a specific person is higher on your priority list than what you were doing before he or she called, politely cut the conversation short and call that person back later at a time more suitable to you. It's that simple.

Suppose people come to you for help when a different problem is already pushing your back to the wall. Do you

- drop everything you were doing and see immediately to their needs?
- ask them to wait a few minutes so you can solve one disaster before rushing off to the next one?
- reexamine your priorities before taking either approach?

There are always catastrophes that demand immediate attention, but under most circumstances, you'll never get anything done if you habitually allow random daily occurrences to supersede your top priorities.

Commit your priority list to writing, update it often, and keep the latest version on the wall, where it will constantly remind you what you have to do. Use big letters and a big message board or easel pad so you can see your priorities from across the room. The list should be a tool to help you allot your time wisely.

Put your personal priorities on there, too. If you don't want others to know what you're up to, write in a cryptic code that will have no meaning to anyone else, and have a simple answer to fall back on when a nosy boss or co-worker asks for a translation.

BLOCK OUT THE HOURS

If you had only one priority, time would be less of a problem and maybe no problem. But you probably always have several high-priority items to take care of. Once you are sure you have identified all priorities for the coming week, determine how many hours or minutes each will take, and block out that time on a calendar.

Rarely can any one priority be met by performing only one activity. Preparing a budget, for example, requires you to take many steps, each demanding a finite amount of your time. You may first have to decide which expense categories to deal with, and then how many dollars should be allocated to each. But before taking these steps, you'll probably have to examine past budgets to determine which categories were previously used and how they were handled.

Not only will you want to establish all the necessary budget numbers, you should check them and use your best desktop-publishing software to prepare any special analyses, graphs, or charts that will make your good work look especially valuable. You might also create a slide presentation to show how your ideas will reduce costs or direct more money into the boss's pet boondoggle or private slush fund. Make a list of all these steps, and set aside a realistic amount of time for each.

Work backward from your deadlines. To make the best impression with that budget proposal you're working on, you've decided to print it in color, but you don't have a color printer. For the proposal to be on your boss's desk by 4 P.M. Thursday, it has to be at the print shop no less than two hours earlier. To get there by 2, however, you have to leave your office by 1:30. That's when you must finish your end of the work. These steps are illustrated in Table VII.

Table VII

Activity	Start time	Finish time
Take budget to print shop	1:30	2:00
Printing	2:00	3:30
Return from print shop	3:30	4:00
Deliver proposal to your boss	4:00	—

If you must perform subsequent activities at different locations, schedule in enough time to travel from place to place. Allow time also for other steps that must take place between activities. Typical examples are waiting for approval, for supplies to be shipped, or for key people to call with information you need. Some people are more cooperative than others, so if you have to deal with someone who rarely gets back to you the day you call, don't get upset at him; get upset at yourself for not taking his lateness in account.

You don't have to complete an activity all at once. If you decide that you need three hours to research previous budgets, you could block out 9 to 12 on Monday morning for that work. Or, you could do it from 9 to 10 on Monday morning, 2 to 2:30 Tuesday afternoon, and 10:30 to 12 Wednesday morning. Activities can overlap or be done piecemeal. The choice is yours and any sequence is okay as long as long as you finish each activity when you need it. In the example shown in Table VII, the proposal must be printed before it can be delivered to the boss.

Don't schedule only through 5 P.M. or 6 P.M. and stop. You may choose to keep your personal, after-hours timetable in a private place, but schedule all around the clock and make sure you allow a few minutes each day for evaluating and updating your plans. Yesterday's priorities may be every bit as useless as yesterday's traffic report.

With a complete schedule, you always know what you're supposed to be doing and where you're supposed to be doing it. But the most important benefit that a schedule can provide is to stir you to action whenever you have set aside time for everybody's priorities but your own. Have you allocated the hours necessary to write that résumé? Observe your boss and determine his needs? Motivate him? Network with your peers? If you haven't scheduled any of these priorities, go back to square one and reblock your time accordingly.

Computerized scheduling software is quite advanced today. Some programs come with built-in alarms to remind you of your goals and obligations each day. If you have never used a schedule rigorously, however, I recommend that you start by putting the public part of your timetable up on the wall right next to your priority list. Aside from constantly reminding you that you don't have time to waste, your schedule will show you where you have time to spare and where you do not.

AVOID SURPRISES

One of the biggest mistakes you can make in managing your time is failing to allow for all the unforeseen meetings, phone calls, and other interruptions that crop up every day. The simplest way to accommodate surprises is to plan for them by building "hedges" into your time blocks. If you are convinced that you can do something in an hour, allow extra time for the unpredictable. Start with thirty minutes of extra time for every hour you think you need. Plan on it. If you don't need the extra time, reschedule and eliminate it. You may improve to the point where you will need only fifteen minutes extra per hour. Perhaps you'll even finish things ahead of time for a change.

TIME TIPS

Force the boss to be his own scapegoat. The next time the boss wants you to sit in on a meeting or take on a new assignment, don't say that you can't. Instead, tell him you'd be happy to help, but doing so would interfere with something else you are already tackling. Who gave you that other priority? He did, so capitalize on the situation. Spin, and don't be timid about it. Emphasize the dangers of postponing the priority you prefer, downgrade the importance of everything else, and let him make the choice.

Let the phone ring. Allow a machine, an answering service, or a secretary to pick up your calls. If none of those options are available and you have no time, just don't answer the ringing phone. If the call is *that* important, the caller will try again later.

Work at home. If nobody is there to bother you, two hours at home can be as productive as six or eight hours in the office.

Hide. Sneak away to an office where people will not easily find you. Better yet, save your work on a notebook computer and go to a park or a hotel lobby. Thousands of people may be there, but none will interrupt you.

Say No. It's hard to say no to the boss, but use him as your scapegoat when saying no to everyone else. Simply tell others that you'd love to help, but your boss has buried you under tons of work that has to be finished immediately.

BE CREATIVE

Damn! You had to call Dennis to get some information, but you had forgotten what a ratchet-jaw that man can be. He just won't stop talking. Yet you need not wreck your schedule. Since you can't tell him to zip it without hurting his feelings, don't say anything once he gives you what you want. Let him blab all he wants, but do something productive in the meanwhile. Read or write a report, while occasionally saying "uh huh" or "mmm." Chances are he won't even know you're not paying attention. You may even benefit by convincing him that you commiserate with his position, even though you were actually figuring out your taxes and ignored at least half of what he said.

Working while on the phone is one of many techniques you can use to get the most out of your time. You can also:

Accomplish something during lunch. Tell me you're not going to waste an entire hour on nothing else but hurling food down your gullet. Surely you can chew and read at the same time. Perhaps you can even swallow and type simultaneously.

Make use of the time wasted by others during meetings. Most business meetings could be over in fewer than thirty minutes, yet they grind on for hour after excruciating hour.

You grow bored and sleepy listening to the unprepared, the inarticulate, and the long-winded. Such meetings waste the company's time, but let the stockholders worry about that. Your worry is that every minute wasted on that meeting adds a minute to the time you're going to have to work at home tonight to make sure you stay on schedule.

You may not be able to recover the time lost at a meeting, but you can always compensate for lots of it by writing furiously while people talk. Bring a notebook, files, and some work you can do without being obvious. Sit across the table from the boss, and off to the side. You don't need him peering over your shoulder or staring at you, wondering what you are doing.

What are you doing—taking notes on what happened at the meeting? Only in the unlikely event that somebody says something of value. The rest of the time, you're going to do something that is highly unusual in meetings. You're going to get something accomplished. Can you proofread those letters you wrote earlier? Update your schedule? Plan that vacation trip you're taking later in the year? Make a list of the bills you have to pay or the calls you have to make? Of course you can. You may also be able to fine-tune that résumé you haven't finished.

Use meetings to observe the people you want to motivate. Even if you can't work during meetings, don't just sit in place listening to others babble. Watch your boss, for example. What upsets him? What kinds of statements and comments turn him off? Who says those things?

Conversely, who pleases him? What kind of things does that person say to him? Find a pattern you can emulate and that meeting will be well worth your time, no matter how unproductive it may otherwise seem.

Make use of commuting time. You may not be able to read documents or use your notebook computer while driving, but you can do some of those things on a train or bus.

Observe and motivate by plan and by schedule, not by accident. I know I've already said this, but it's worth repeating. Schedule time to have dinner with the boss, or to drive with him to and from that meeting across town. You can also plan what to discuss during these activities. Have an agenda prepared for yourself, but don't forget to schedule enough time to prepare that agenda.

NO EXCEPTIONS

What you do with your time is up to you, not me. I am telling you only that if something is important to you, put it on your schedule and spare as much time for it as you can, depending upon how high a priority it is. Do *not,* however, spend one minute more than that on it. You may need that minute for something else.

............12............

Performance Reviews

Performance reviews are meetings during which you and your boss are supposed to discuss your achievements for the year gone by and to agree on your goals, plans, and compensation for the year to come. That's a charming idea, but it has nothing to do with reality. The usual review, you see, is not a review at all, and it certainly isn't a place for salary negotiations. It's a post-mortem.

Most employees deal with reviews in a simple, unproductive way. Throughout the year, they do their work without thinking of their next review. Then, a day or two before that review, they decide on what they see as a persuasive argument to convince the boss that he should jack up their income or give them whatever else they might want. I'd like to tell you that they succeed, but I can't, because they don't. You can't expect to get a raise or anything else by doing nothing except preparing a clever "sales pitch" the day before a review. What will you do, appeal to the boss's sympathy? His sense of justice? You might as well talk to a tree.

This is because bosses usually don't enter reviews with an open mind. Most reviews occur after a boss has already determined what rewards he will give you for the year gone by. By the time you meet with him, he has already decided what he wants to do.

But that doesn't mean you're sunk. Not at all. There's still a lot you can do. But you can't wait until just prior to your next review. Start immediately after your last review. Observe, test, and scratch that boss's back as diligently as you can; every day of the week, every week of the year. Motivate to the extent that there's no way he could forget or disregard what you have done for him. But that isn't all. Don't sit down and rest; motivating is only your first step. The next steps are as follows.

PUT THE BOSS ON NOTICE

The comedian Milton Berle was famous for the rapid-fire jokes on his television show years ago. One of my favorites was:

"Don't applaud, folks. Just throw money."

That may not be especially funny, but it's a great reference to reality. I'm certain that Mr. Berle knew that if audiences did not applaud, television networks would never have paid him much. I'm big on the value of applauding an employee's work by saying "thanks," but I have no use for empty thanks.

Your boss has applauded you for doing something well and thanked you for your hard work. Isn't that nice? Of course it is. You should show your appreciation and tell him that he is welcome, but you should not ask him to hold the applause and throw money at you. However, you can take a page from Milton Berle's book, put a smile on your face, and laughingly say something like:

"Thanks, does this mean I'm getting a big raise this year?"

Too bold for you? How about:

*"Thanks. I hope you remember this
when my review comes up."*

If you made a habit of saying this, its effectiveness would wear thin, but if you find yourself being thanked *that* effusively, give it a try on occasion. It's not so strong that it is likely to create antagonism, but it will show him that you appreciate his thoughts. It will also show that you *do* think about being thanked in concrete terms.

FIRE THE OPENING SALVO

Take a few minutes each Friday to make a list of everything you have done to scratch backs during the week that just ended. For each item listed, indicate the date, how your good work benefited the company, and how it benefited the boss. One such listing might look something like the entries in Table VIII.

As you make up your list, be certain to include notation of any occasion on which you received praise, thanks, or congratulations, especially if it came from your boss. You may need a stack of such notations to offset any contention the boss makes to the effect that your performance was unsatisfactory.

Table VIII. TYPICAL WEEKLY BACK-SCRATCHING/APPLAUSE LIST

Item	Date	Benefits to company	Benefits to Boss
Wrote Joule Publications Proposal	4/15	Million-dollar order	He shares credit for booking the order
Explanation for the Manor problem	4/16	None	Design flaw blamed on consultant
Hired R.W.	4/17	Good programmer	R.W. willing to work cheap
Thank-you letter from A.G. Corporation	4/17	Efforts are recognized by major customer	You shared the credit with him
Suggested that ad budget be cut	4/18	Saves money	Looks like a good manager or gets to keep the saved money for himself
Lunch; listened to his story about problems with his doctor	4/18	None	You listened. No one else did
Boss congratulates you on meeting your March goals	4/18	Work gets done on time	He looks like a good manager
Volunteered to tell J.T. the bad news about his request for help	4/19	None	He avoids the unpleasantries
Compliance reports are done on time and under boss's signature	4/19	Meets contractual obligations	He looks like a good manager

Every item in your list need not be monumental. When you put fifty-two lists together, the effect is cumulative. What's important is that by the time you have your performance review, you are armed with specific times, dates, achievements, and all the good results stemming from those achievements.

When you want something from your boss, study your weekly lists. Cull them to come up with a separate list of the top ten things you have done since the last review that directly and personally benefit the boss. Make it a top-twenty list if you like.

Rewrite the list so you could show it to the boss without causing him to take offense. He may not, for example, want to give you a raise for being the employee who kept him from making a fool of himself during that big contract dispute in January. Your list can, however, point out that you supported his efforts throughout that episode and also that he thanked you accordingly. Similarly, anything you did to allay his fears would be best presented as action you took to "ensure the success of our program."

Once the list is so prepared, give it a title indicating that it summarizes your recent accomplishments. As you're doing that, make up a second list, this time mentioning the most glowing compliments or thanks you have received for a job well done, particularly if your boss was the source. Call that one your praises list.

Don't wait until a performance review to show the boss your top-ten or top-twenty lists. Take action whenever you want your performance reviewed. You do not have to wait for a boss to schedule a review. You know when the last one took place; no more than eleven months later, send the boss a brief memo asking when he can meet with you to review your performance. Enclose your top-ten accomplishments list and your top ten praises lists. By sending him your lists in advance, you not only remind him of your value, you head off

any attempt he may make to shaft you by bringing up performance "deficiencies" he has not mentioned beforehand.

WATCH OUT FOR DELAYING TACTICS

Your boss may be in no hurry to "review" your performance,
much less to reward you. He may try to postpone any meeting
and then to spring it on you without warning. If he succeeds,
he gives himself the upper hand because he leaves you with no
opportunity to get emotionally prepared for battle. You may
have experienced one or more of several ploys that bosses use
in this regard. They will:

- delay a performance review any number of times, supposedly because various crises came up requiring their
immediate attention.
- delay the meeting a few more times because they allegedly
weren't able to consult with their bosses beforehand.
- suggest a time that will not give you an ample opportunity to discuss things. If they have a visitor coming at 3
P.M., for example, bosses may ask to meet with you at
2:30 and then cut you off before you have had a chance
to express yourself.
- promise you great rewards if you will agree to meet at a
later date, when the climate for a raise would supposedly
be better.

Whichever of these schemes a boss uses, don't believe him
if he reschedules your review more than once or twice. Your
daughter's college tuition may be on the line, but to the boss,
delaying a review is merely a tactic in a sick game designed
to make sure that you get as little as possible. Don't accept

any delays without insisting on setting a specific "rain date," and don't get sucked into meeting at an inconvenient time.

If you wish, you can give him your own pile of excuses. Tell him you're fighting a deadline, that there isn't enough time to complete your discussion with him before his (or your) next meeting, or anything else that will sound advantageous to him.

I know one person who, upon being invited to a surprise review, went so far as to claim that an upset stomach cause him to "lose his lunch" in his lap. Saying that he was afraid it might happen again, he asked for his review to be put off until the next day. A bit bizarre? It was *extremely* bizarre, but it worked. This character will never get awards for class, but the only prize he wanted right then was to meet at a time of his own choosing. And in no way did that boss want his office messed up.

Your boss will probably agree to delays for seemingly good reasons, but he may ask for alternate dates. Say that you'll check your schedule and get back to him. Then, try to catch *him* off guard. Pop in on him unannounced and see whether he can meet with you immediately. You may never take him completely by surprise, but that's less important than making sure that you are in the right mood to meet with him.

MORE PLOYS

It's hard to make a point with someone when he or she is yelling at you or threatening to fire you. Bosses know this. They also know that many people are terrified at the thought of asking for a raise or expressing dissatisfaction with the way they have been treated. To take advantage of these feelings, they'll do almost anything to give themselves the upper hand by making performance reviews as confrontational and intimidating as possible. Even after agreeing to meet with you, they may:

- begin your review by claiming to be in an ugly mood because of some offense that others have committed against him. What he wants, of course, is to cow you into feeling that you should not be too aggressive.
- suggest again that you delay your performance review until the company's financial health is better.
- put on a show of apparent outrage the second that you ask for anything. He may not say no, but he will seem to be quite upset at your joining the chorus of voices he claims is trying to take the shirt off his back. Once again, this is a show designed to keep you from becoming too pushy.
- start the meeting by telling you how terrible sales or profits have been.
- "hide" behind a big desk while you sit across the room in a chair with nothing in front of it, not even a writing surface. He'll kick off his shoes and be comfortable, but you're exposed, so to speak. He would probably be more at ease than you in that circumstance, therefore holding an advantage over you.
- take notes, particularly after you make statements or answer questions. This is designed to make you uncomfortable by wondering what he is writing about you, and what those notes will be used for.
- allow the meeting to be interrupted by telephone calls and also by people coming in with questions.
- attempt to schmooze even though you are trying to get to the point.
- give you a lecture on the importance of teamwork and then claim to be insulted about your lack of concern for

the company's financial health if you protest the measly nature of your raise.

- accuse you of having a "bad" attitude if you get upset about being passed over for a raise or a promotion.

All these ploys have a great deal in common. Their purpose is to fight your attempts at getting rewarded. They're manipulative, they're designed to put you at a disadvantage, and many of them are gross misrepresentations of the truth, if not outright lies. Yes, it's possible that the company is broke and that you're incompetent, but it's also possible that the next stranger you meet will be twelve feet tall and have five eyes.

FIGHT BACK

The boss is throwing everything in his arsenal at you. First he hits you with a withering barrage of excuses to avoid the review process altogether, and then he lets loose with additional firepower to avoid compensating you to the extent that you would like. I hope you are not going to let him get away with it without a fight.

Politely decline if a boss asks you to put off a performance review until the climate for raises is better. Tell him that you will gladly accept any conditional promises he can make, but that you really do want to meet now.*

Before you go to the review, be sure you are well dressed, groomed, and coiffed. If you look less than completely professional, he will treat you as less than completely professional. Bring a notebook, make your own notes, and let *him* wonder what they're for.

---

*Accepting the existence of a promise is not the same as believing its contents.

Once you enter the boss's office, make yourself as comfortable as he is, but do not slump or fidget. Look at him right between the eyes when you talk. If he is behind a desk with his papers close at hand, sit immediately on the other side of that desk and take all the room you need to write your notes.

Then, if you think that he is throwing too many delaying/distraction tactics at you, beg off and bail out. You don't have to sit there and fight your way through a conversation cut short by phone calls, phony fits of anger, conversations that sidetrack you, and excuses that are dredged up from no place just to diminish your focus.

Make your move the minute you sense that this may be happening. Tell him that you have headaches or back pains. Alternatively, you might excuse yourself to check on some "emergency" and come back a couple of minutes later claiming that you have to run off to slay a dragon someplace. This is another time planning will come in handy. Have a story prepared. Complete with dragon, it should put you in an ideal position to duck out and explain yourself away.

One guy I used to work with once called his wife right before he had a performance review. About twenty minutes later, he received an "urgent" call from a voice no one recognized.* The interrupting call gave my friend the option to continue or reschedule, depending on how well he thought the review was progressing.

*His wife asked her out-of-town brother to place the call.

ALLEGED DEFICIENCIES

After giving you nothing but compliments all year, your boss tells you that everything you do is sloppy and that he has heard others offer similar criticisms. He says you have made expensive mistakes. While you are trying to figure out what he is talking about and who could have leveled such preposterous condemnations at you, things get worse. He says that your deficiencies are hurting the company's (or the department's) reputation, and that he's not sure whether he can keep you on board, much less give you a raise.

Suddenly, instead of negotiating for a higher salary, you find yourself fighting for your job. He says he's under pressure from his bosses to fire you. You protest, but he persists. You ask for an explanation. He angrily spouts out one or two examples where he claims you have screwed up. You say he is misinformed, but he jabs at you mercilessly. You plead some more, he hems and haws, and you promise that he'll have no more problems with you. In the end, he magnanimously agrees to give you one more chance to redeem yourself.

You leave feeling as you have avoided a catastrophe. He feels the same way, but to him a catastrophe would have been giving you a decent raise. Ten minutes after you leave his office, he's laughing, but you're not.

I hope this vignette hasn't hit too close to home. If it has, chances are you've been had; taken in by one of the oldest scams in the management book. It's one thing to discuss problems that you recognize, but when they have never been mentioned before and then all of a sudden they become a disaster, you should be suspicious. "If I'm that bad," you should ask yourself, "why didn't anybody say anything earlier?" I'll tell you why. Nobody said anything earlier because nobody was trying to divert your attention from pressing for a raise or some other form of job satisfaction.

Keep your focus, stay calm, don't get defensive, and do *not* allow this to happen. Instead of allowing trumped-up "problems" to distract you from focusing on your accomplishments, be assertive. Pull out your top-ten list. Reiterate your achievements one by one. Be specific, citing not only what you did but the date on which you did it. Go through your praises list and remind him of any occasions on which he had nice words to say about your work.

Ask questions. What mistakes did you make? When did you make them? What problems did they cause? What should you have done that you didn't do? Listen carefully to the answers you get, and write everything down in your notebook for future reference. Unless those answers are highly specific at every step of the way, you're getting double-talked at every step of the way.

Avoid being defensive in reviews, and behave as if you genuinely want to make things better. Ask more questions. What do you have to do to improve in the boss's eyes? Will he help you? How? Will he meet with you in two or three months for another review? Tell him that you wouldn't want to waste a whole year going in the wrong direction. Once again, write his answers in your notebook.

Two results will ensue from all this. If his complaints are valid, he will give you specifics to make things better, he will agree to help, and he will express a willingness to meet with you again soon to make sure you are headed in the right direction. If his complaints are all smoke and mirrors, on the other hand, chances are he will not be prepared for your questions. He may get angry if you persist, but what do you have to lose? He's getting a great deal of back-scratching from you. He won't walk away from that so quickly. Continue pressing him to meet again with you in a few weeks or a few months.

"WE CAN'T AFFORD IT."

One of the world's largest companies recently announced that it was laying off thousands of employees. Apparently the company couldn't afford to keep all those people on the payroll any longer. A few weeks later word leaked out that the same company was giving its chief executive a megamillion-dollar bonus equal to twice what was saved by the layoffs. You can judge for yourself the depth of that executive's actual concern for the company's stockholders.

Pity the plight of the typical CEO. The miserable SOB can afford a generous raise only for himself, and then he has to gall to complain that his job is tough and that it's "lonely at the top." Of course it's lonely. Almost everyone else has been laid off. Those who are left get nothing more than a pat on the back and a whopper of a story about having to wait for a raise until business improves.

I tend not to believe those stories. You'd be amazed how much a company can afford when the big boss wants to stuff his pockets. To show what bosses want to show, accountants can "cook the books" and play wonders with corporate profit-and-loss statements. This is why bosses are so smug when they thank you for your good work and say that as much as they'd like to give you a raise, they can't afford to do so.

Please understand; I am never shocked when people put themselves first. That's survival instinct, pure and simple. Neither am I upset about the unfairness of management in taking all the spoils for themselves and convincing everyone else that there's no money for raises. If I let them con me like that, it's my fault, not theirs.

Table IX. WISH-LIST ITEMS AND THEIR JUSTIFICATIONS

What you want	Real reason for wanting it	Reason you give the boss
Several tall filing cabinets	He wouldn't give you a private office, so you'll build one with a wall of filing cabinets	Your area will be neater and free of clutter. You could be faster in finding the documents he wants
Cellular phone	Instead of your having to lay out money for calls, the phone bill goes to the company	He could find you faster when you are traveling
To join a trade association	You want to network for job possibilities	You would be better able to keep tabs on competitors
To go to the big trade show	It's the perfect place to look for a new job	You would brief him on customer/competitor trends
All employees to get written list of job responsibilities	He keeps on claiming that you are supposed to do things he never told you to do	He'll be better able to pin people down
To attend some of the meetings your boss has with the CEO	To increase your exposure to top management	You'll stay abreast of plans and programs without having to pester him
A new desk and chair	Yours is beat-up and depressing to look at every morning	Suggest that he get new furniture, and point out how little it would cost to set you up similarly

More decision-making latitude	You're sick of being treated like a child
	If you had a yearly (or even monthly) budget, he would retain control, but you wouldn't have to take up his time every time you had to make a decision
A paint job in your office	The place is dingy and dreary. Only the cockroaches like the ambiance
	Customers cringe at having to visit you. And, while the painters were in, his office could also be done
Staff meetings first thing Monday morning, not 6 P.M.	You want a life, not just a job
	The end-of-day time interferes with business trips. More people could attend more regularly if you held the meeting first thing Monday mornings
A fancier job title (such as Sales VP rather than Sales Manager)	May look better on your résumé*
	Gives your word more credibility with customers
A company car	Yours is falling apart
	With your mileage, the cost would be minimal
A better parking space	Yours may not be in the next county, but it is at the far end of the company parking lot
	You could run his errands faster if you didn't have to walk twenty minutes to reach your car
Performance reviews quarterly rather than once a year	To avoid surprises the boss may spring on you in a performance appraisal
	You could more closely monitor your performance and make more timely adjustments in your ways

*Job titles can also hurt if you're not careful. See page 179.

GIVE THE BOSS YOUR "WISH LIST"

Go back to Table II in chapter 2. What are the primary reasons for your lack of job satisfaction? Aside from discovering
that someone dropped an anvil on your boss's head from an
altitude of several thousand feet, what else could make you
happy? Write it down, figure out a way to ask for it in a way
that highlights the benefits the boss will derive, and put it on a
"wish list" of results you might realistically expect from your
review. Leave out the diamond tiara and the Jaguar convert-
ible. I said *wish* list, not wild dream list.

Your boss is no doubt talented and brilliant, a wonderful
person admired by one and all. That's what he thinks. You
may have other descriptions in mind for him, but let's skip
those for now. I'm sure the two of you agree on some things,
one of which is that he is not a mind reader. He can give you
what you want only if he knows what that is. He may not ask
what that is, so you'll have to tell him.

If what you want is a raise, say how much. As long as what
you ask for is reasonable, there's nothing wrong with being
open about it. Don't be surprised, however, if your boss
throws the can't-afford-it excuse in your face.

Bosses may be able to use that excuse for not giving you a
raise, but affordability has no meaning on items that either
cost little or save money in the long run. I'll bet you have several wants like that. If you present them as benefiting him
without robbing him of his power, his glory, or his money,
you just may get them. This is the beauty of coming to a performance review with a "wish list" that goes beyond your
salary requirements.

Particularly good candidates for your wish list are any items
on which you can use spin to show how your boss will benefit
if you get what you want. You might, for example, want a new

computer to replace one that's cumbersome and slow. But convenience is a reason that appeals to *you*. Come up with one that appeals to the *boss*. Show him how a new computer would enable you to do certain items of work by yourself instead of subcontracting them outside of the company. Show him how much he is spending on that outside work, and give him calculations proving that the new computer would soon pay for itself if you did the work in-house. Don't say anything about the added job security you might gain.

What else? Some possibilities are listed in Table IX.

The logic behind some of the justifications in Table IX might be a stretch for your boss's imagination, but that's okay. If you hear a "can't afford it" story that stretches your imagination, tell him about your wish list. Don't call it that, just say that in light of his financial problems, perhaps he can reward you in other ways. Give him five or six items from the top of your list. Asking for too much may turn him off completely, and he may at any time realize exactly what you're up to. If your "justifications" are strong enough, however, he may just see your list as an inexpensive way to appease you.

The items on your wish list may not make up for a lack of money. They might add to your job satisfaction if you get them, however, and they won't hurt. Put together your own list. Make it as long as you wish. If your accomplishments and praises lists are even longer, you'll probably get a lot more than nothing.

STILL MORE PLOYS

Playing the wish-list game in reverse, some bosses will attempt to mollify you with rewards that are all form and no substance. A typical ruse in this respect is a company car or new office furniture. The furniture can be nice, but cars may involve hidden costs. Your boss may let you use that fancy roadster, but if you have to pay for insurance and gas, operating costs may be much higher than those of your subcompact. Be careful about any compensation that is less than what you wanted, that makes life more expensive for you, or that diverts your focus from your real goals.

The first time a boss offered me a promotion to company vice president, he rambled on for more than half an hour about the great opportunity he was giving me. It was clear, however, that the man was giving me nothing but the chance to have a fancier title on my business card. I declined his generosity, saying only that I preferred my current job. If only to enhance my résumé, perhaps I should have accepted his offer, but I allowed that boss to sidetrack my focus.

Maybe it's just as well. I didn't know then that high-level titles are not always good on résumés. Sometimes they can actually hurt. The same job title is likely to have different meanings at different companies. Some sales vice presidents, for example, are sales managers with a fancy title, while others are true corporate officers. Employers seeking a sales manager may mistakenly decline to interview someone who is now a sales VP, assuming that he or she would want "too much" money or "too much" power.

Divulging your salary might seem like a way to circumvent the title problem, but it isn't. You'll never get an interview if you show a current salary that's well above a boss's budget.* You may not want to take a pay cut, but who says you should? If you have a VP title, use it on résumés only when applying for VP jobs. Otherwise, use a less lofty manager title, highlight how successful you have been, and at

---

*You'll also probably not get an interview if your income is well below what employers want to pay. They'll think there's something wrong with you.

least stick your foot in the door. If you get that far, maybe you can spin your way up to the pay you want.

SPEAK UP

As soon as bosses see that they can stiff you and get away with it, they'll do it every time. You may not be able to retaliate, and you may not even want to do so, but you should speak up immediately and express your pain in a way that lets them know that you are not pleased with their story.

Once you agree to a certain salary level one week, you will lose all credibility if you come back the next week or the next month and ask for more. Unless the floodgates have been opened wide and most generously for you, I suggest that you voice any reservations you may have on your boss's offering. You may have to go along with it temporarily, but you don't have to say that you like it.

To the contrary, you have everything to gain by letting your boss know exactly what you think of how he is treating you. Well, maybe not exactly. Be diplomatic. Don't accuse him of lying or of being the swamp rat that he is. Say that you

- understand his position, but do not agree with it and do not like it.
- will take what he is offering, but only for now in the anticipation that things will get better "in the *very* near future."
- think the whole situation stinks!

On the matter of alleged deficiencies that were just brought to your attention for the first time, deny them—vehemently. If what he claims is so horrible, you can ask, why did he never say anything beforehand? Then, instead of being drawn into a confrontation, point to your praises list. Ask him how he can forget all the times he had nice things to say about you, and instead focus on other "problems" that he has never mentioned. If he doesn't budge, look right at him , and in the sternest, most serious voice you can muster, say that the situation is *not* acceptable.

I'm tempted to tell you not to yell or scream, but those tactics can work. I have personally seen more than one powerful, overbearing male executive back down completely when confronted by a tiny female who became furious upon hearing that her wages were being frozen. In each instance, the look on his face must have been exactly what it had been years earlier when his mother scolded him for being a bad boy.

You don't have to tell me that speaking up is difficult. I know it is. However, bullies and con artists will thrive on you if you do not speak up. They want a confrontation no more than anyone else, so they pick on the easiest targets. When someone does fight back, they hate it and they'll often back down rather than lose outright. But "often" is not "always," so don't get carried away. Perhaps the most prudent advice I can give you about speaking up is to reread chapter 7 and take your stand on principles.

BE TENACIOUS

Your review is about to end. You are not at all satisfied and you have clearly said so to the boss. But don't stop there. Press him for the answers to four questions:

1. What has to happen before you can get what you want?
2. How long does he think that might take?

3. How, if you do make changes, will you be able to tell whether they are to his satisfaction?
4. Can you speak with him in a few weeks to check on your progress?
5. Ask whether there are any ways that you can make his job (or his life) easier by assuming more responsibilities or by helping him to do his work. He may not open up to you, but he may give you some important clues on new ways by which you can scratch his back.

If he gets defensive or skittish, tell him that you would like his help to do a better job and that you hope he'll have the time to give you that help. Ask him to be as specific as possible so you can better gauge how you stand. Is he looking to triple profitability before he can justify giving you a raise, or would a 30 percent improvement be a good start in the short term? Does he want you to cut your budget by 50 percent, or would he be happy with a 10 percent reduction? These are not unreasonable questions. Press him for answers, write down those answers, and remember not to patronize or interrogate him.

PUT IT IN WRITING

People have a habit of remembering every last detail of your promises to them, while forgetting much of what they have promised to you. This is nothing personal. Those who do it to you probably do it to everybody.

The ideal way to deal with selective memories is to get people to document their promises to you, but this poses another problem. As soon as you ask someone to "put it in writing," however, he may take offense in your not accepting his word or his handshake. Whether rational or not, his indignation will quickly replace protecting your interests as the focus of the conversation.

But he's not the only one who can write. You do the writing. A week or two after your performance review, send your boss a right-to-the-point memo saying that you appreciate his advice, and that you thank him for agreeing to meet with you in a few weeks to give you his opinion on how you are doing in improving your performance to his satisfaction. If he made any specific promises to you, document them in the memo and ask him to let you know if you have misunderstood him.

Rather than trying to remember his words months later, you know exactly what he said because you wrote it down when he said it. More important, he knows it too.

FOLLOW UP

If your boss uses the "can't afford it" story on you, watch what happens as time goes on. Does the company land a huge order that will obviously turn profits upward? Another sign to look for is large expenses. If the company is suddenly spending lots of money, speak up.

But don't ask for a raise just then. That will put your boss on the defensive, much in the manner of a wounded tiger. Just send him a memo asking him to meet with you to discuss your "situation." Don't tell him anything else. He'll know that you are concerned about something, but your memo doesn't say what that something is, so he'll have to talk with you to find out.

By the way, if the boss engages in more delaying tactics when you ask for a meeting, wait a little while, switch gears, and suggest that he join you for lunch one day. Don't say anything about wanting an interim performance review. It's just lunch, and just the two of you. After you sit down, schmooze for a few minutes, and then ask him how you have been doing. If he is complimentary, ask how you can do even more, but keep the conversation low key. Assuming that the lunch is a success, try it again in a month. If he is still pleased and he stops using the "can't afford it" nonsense, ask him again for whatever it was that he couldn't afford to give you during your review. If he turns you down, ask why and keep on asking why.

Another possibility is to take the boss by surprise when you meet with him alone on a business matter. Before you get to what he wants to discuss, catch him off guard by talking about your review. Remind him that the company's fortunes were in terrible shape back then. Read from your notebook, as if to quote his implication that he would review things again if the economic climate improved.

Don't make demands, but tell him that you have been happy to see the new influx of business and the new spending plans. Ask him whether positive changes have indeed come about. If he says they have, ask for another review immediately. If he again says that he'd prefer to wait, try once more in a few weeks, and press even harder. Don't let him forget for a moment that you continue to be upset.

DON'T WAIT

There is no reason why you should wait twelve months or more for a performance review. I see no reason for waiting more than one month. Try some changes, continue scratching his back, and if you want a review right away, go for it right away. If not for a raise, at the least to check with him to get his views on whether that you are going in the right direction.

Your boss may resist, so you may have to ask again. How often is a function of how much of a pest you think you can make of yourself before you do yourself more harm than good. How often is that? I don't know. That depends on how much tolerance your boss has, and also on how much guts you have. Be persistent, but remember that your objective is to motivate the boss to be nice to you, not to think of you as an annoyance.

A FEW ROTTEN APPLES

As I have been telling you all along, doing a good job is never enough. You have to scratch backs, too. If you do, most bosses will scratch yours in return. They're not likely to empty their pockets or their jewelry boxes in your lap, but you won't have to prod them to take good care of you. Others will resist, but they'll step up their efforts on your behalf when you confront them with your accomplishments and praises lists and make it clear that you're not satisfied with the status quo.

How hard do your bosses try to comply with your overall wish list? The company really may have financial problems, and higher-level bosses may be the actual culprits who are clamping down on raises. Your own bosses may not always be able to give you everything you want, but the good ones will look closely at your wish list and find ways to prevent you from leaving a review empty-handed. Their efforts will be obvious, and they will do whatever they can on your behalf; not necessarily because they are fair, but because they are selfish and want more of the same from you.

Regardless of how hard you work or how much you accomplish on their behalf, however, some people won't even try to treat you equitably. There will always be a few rotten apples who will either pay no attention to you, refuse to trust you, or go out of their way to shaft you.

Typically, these ingrates insist on thinking that only they are important. Resistant to the idea that your assistance has been important to them, they are likely to scream and bellow at you if you pressure them too hard for any sort of additional compensation. A few may even take your back-scratching as a sign of weakness. With no intention of reciprocating, they may try to goad you into doing even more for them.

Confronting any of them is risky indeed, but what should you do—fold up your tent, forget your dreams, and give up on your goals? No. Don't ever do that. If you follow every bit of advice I've given to this point and you still don't have the job satisfaction you'd like, you still have some other options. You'll find them described in the next two chapters.

····· **13** ·····

Alternatives

Look once again at Table II in chapter 2. What did you say is lacking about your job? Think of each deficiency as an ingredient in a recipe for satisfaction. No matter which missing ingredient might be most important to you, instead of looking to your job for it, and rather than giving up on it because there are no better jobs available, you should seek out and find alternate ways to get it.

The more sources you have for income, for example, the less you must rely on your job for money. This is difficult, but many people do it, some with part-time jobs, some with part-time businesses, and some with both. But we've already talked (in chapter 3) about alternate ways to make money. Now, let's find substitute means for meeting the other needs that you have looked to your job to supply.

SELF-RESPECT

This is the most important need we have. If you don't like yourself or what you are doing, you're going to be dissatisfied no matter how much money you are making and regardless of who else praises you. If you are unhappy in your job and do nothing about it, you'll be out-and-out miserable.

Any incremental progress you make in diminishing your reliance on a terrible job will provide you with potentially massive improvements in your self-esteem. Five or 10 percent more money from an extracurricular venture might not sound like much, but if you couple it with any extra enjoyment or challenge you get, you're going to feel a whole lot better. And I don't mean by only 5 or 10 percent.

FULFILLMENT

You take a job, it's fun, it makes use of your skills, and you enjoy it. One, two, or five years down the road, however, you will have done every part of that job a thousand times over. What was interesting when you started will become routine, and you will get bored—terribly bored. Even if your boss kicks in with a nice raise, the work won't be any less tedious. The longer you continue on that job, the more you're going to hate it.

But what about the rest of your life? I don't mean after you retire. I'm talking about after dinner. You can often offset, if not completely overcome, a lack of fulfillment at work by adding challenge and gratification to other aspects of your life. Writing helped me do this.

Twenty years ago I was advertising manager at a company

run by an egomaniacal windbag who criticized everything I did, refused to approve any of my work without gratuitous revisions, and once threatened to fire me unless I took a course in effective writing. He never knew that I was at the same time starting a thriving career as a writer. I had had one book published, had a contract in hand for a second book, and was teaching business writing at four colleges. Not eager to live in the street, I was forced to tolerate that jerk's nonsense for a couple of years.

Fortunately, my job took 50 hours a week, tops, and only a part of that was spent arguing with him. The total week has 168 hours, of which I spent 40 sleeping. Take away work and sleep and I was still left with 78 hours to use as I liked. I had other obligations, but I made up my mind to spend more of my waking hours fulfilled than unfulfilled. I did it, but it was hard work. I actually had to forego watching certain sitcoms on television. Other than that, I was doing what I wanted to do, and I was having fun.

My story is not at all unique. A friend of mine sold clothing during the day while he went to law school at night. Another friend runs a fork truck in a warehouse so he can afford to spend the rest of his time as a musician. But don't think for a moment that you need a particular skill to be creative and to do enjoyable work. You need only a brain.

As you may have already discovered, however, you won't always be given credit for having a brain. Your boss may for any number of reasons refuse to give you credit for anything, but does that mean you have to be bored and wasted until he keels over or you find another job? Not at all. Once you walk out the door at the end of the day, you can pursue all sorts of gratification.

One way is to join a club, a civic association, a political party, a professional society, or a charity. Give freely of your time and get active, but avoid groups run by cliques of insiders. They will fight to retain power, and working with them will be just as bad as reporting to an oppressive boss. Look for organizations that are receptive to newcomers who want to take charge, accept responsibility, and make an immediate contribution.

Volunteering can also meet other needs you might have difficulty fulfilling through your work. One such need is a source of friends. Other needs you may have are for status, the respect of others, and the self-esteem one gets from making a difference in the world.

George Rose resented not being allowed to use his talents or to make a simple decision at work without getting permission from his boss. I used to hate talking to George. Every conversation with him centered around how terrible his job was. He was also unfulfilled at home. After a friend spent months urging him to do something productive with his time, George volunteered for a seat on his town's zoning board.

The board met just once a month, but George thought it might give him something to do away from his job. At first, he found the business of government terribly mundane. After the third or fourth meeting, however, George realized that although zoning was never going to be exciting, it was both needed and valuable. His initial bad reaction to it arose from his distaste for the high-handed ways of one Joe Francis, a stuffy old goat who had run the board for years and looked on it as his property.

George complained to the mayor, who pointed out that the only reason Francis had stayed in charge over the years was that no one else had ever campaigned for the post. Mr. Francis had long been a thorn in the mayor's side, and George didn't have to be whacked over the head to take a hint. Soon after the next election he became the new chairman.

Big deal, you say? Maybe not to you, but it turned out to be just that to George. The mayor declined to run for reelection last year, and George became the candidate in his place. The voters went for him by a 3 to 2 majority. George never left his job, but instead of looking on it as his sole means of support and fulfillment, he sees it now as a way to supplement his income. He enjoys life, and working in the community has put him in touch with people who respect him. He says that even his boss voted for him.

I can't tell you whether involvement in government or any other particular activity is your answer. Maybe it isn't. But I can say with certainty that you will never know unless you try. Perhaps you should formalize some hobby you have enjoyed all along. If you have a special car, join a car club, and if you are into computers, get involved in a users' group. Run for office in the PTA. If you feel particularly energetic, do all of these, and don't depend on any one aspect of your life— certainly not your job—to meet 100 percent of any of your needs.

APPROVAL

One of the strangest (and strongest) of human needs is the need for approval. We sometimes want the most approval from people we like the least. That boss you love to hate may be making you unhappy simply by withholding his approval from you.

No matter how much you can't stand someone on a personal level, you may thirst for his approval if you respect him professionally. The more difficult he is to please, the more you feel compelled to try, the more you hate him when he refuses to recognize your good work, and the more dissatisfied you become every time he neglects you or seems to do so. The whole thing is a vicious cycle that continuously feeds on itself.

To make things worse, the problem may persist even if you leave for another job. Having been frustrated at your attempts to make one boss happy, you may try all the harder to please your new one. If the second boss is as difficult as the first, however, you'll remain unsatisfied no matter how much you are paid. You may subconsciously look for the same kind of impossible boss on each new job, just because you desperately need approval from certain types of authority figures.

Approval has different meanings to different people. You may think of what I've been describing as validation or respect more than approval, and that's okay. What's not okay is becoming obsessed with it. That would be illogical. But we are dealing with emotions here, not logic. Approval is a form of ego gratification, and if you can't get it from one person, your next best bet is to get it from so many others that no one individual will matter that much.

Once again, outside affiliations may help. A group unrelated to your work might be of value to you, but for approval on a professional level, try a trade association or chamber of commerce—something you could justify to your boss as relevant to your job. I suggested this in chapter 12 as an entry on a performance review "wish list" you prepare to tell your boss how you'd like to be rewarded for your hard work, but you can discuss membership with him at any time. Tell him that by schmoozing with customers or others in your industry, you can better fill him in on competitive, economic, or technological trends. He may not buy your story, but if he does, perhaps he will lay out your costs.

Once you join, get active and see what the group offers to members who will accept responsibility. Look for things that no one else wants to do. Do those and they'll love you. Well, maybe they won't love you, but they certainly will respect and approve of you.

Regularly report back to the boss, but spend most of your

trade association time working on your own behalf. Submit an article to the monthly magazine or newsletter. Write even if you don't want to be a writer. Seeing your name in print is a great ego booster. So is hearing applause. Prepare a talk about an efficient way you do something at work. If an audience likes you, you'll like yourself, too, and everybody will win.

The more active you become, the more you can position yourself to be thanked and told that you did a good job. The more that happens, the more you can show the rest of the world how good you are. This is networking and schmoozing on a grand scale. It is what many people do to establish reputations, and it is how some people get consideration for job openings that have not yet been advertised.

Lest you think otherwise, bosses need approval, too. The most self-reliant bosses often have the deepest craving for approval. Not only do they like your praise, they need it and they can't do without it. Then again, if they get more from someone else than they get from you, maybe they *can* do without you.

IDENTITY

Some years ago I was house hunting with the help of a real estate agent who asked me what I did for a living. I should have said that I worked in corporate marketing, but my ego spoke up and announced my job title, which was Marketing Vice President. A few minutes later, I was being shown the homes for sale in the neighborhood where corporate executives buy them. Everything there was way above my budget. Quickly realizing what had happened, I asked to be taken to the "middle management" section of town. Once we got there, we found several properties that were more realistically priced for me.

My mistake was in defining myself by my job title rather than by the details of what I wanted. Unfortunately, I'm not alone. What do you say when you meet a stranger who asks "What do you do?" You may be a parent, a child, a golfer, a good friend, an avid reader of Civil War histories, an expert peeler of potatoes, and a respected member of your neighborhood association, but chances are that you'd identify the work you do. You might say that's what people really want to know when they ask what you do, but that isn't the point. We all identify ourselves by our work. I do it too. We are what we do for a living, and when we're out of work, we feel empty and aimless, as if we have no identity.

If you hate your job or your profession, get into the habit of making a little joke when you are asked what you do. Answer first by saying that you do as little as possible. Tell people what your work is, if you like, but follow that up with something you are proud of outside of work:

I'm an engineer, but my passion is classical music.

If you have nothing to brag about just yet, that's okay. Identify what you are by talking about a goal:

I'm going for my master's degree.

This is defining yourself by where you want to be, rather than by where you are at the moment. There is nothing wrong with being a welder, a cab driver, an accountant, or even a lawyer. There's nothing wrong with any profession if you like it. If you want to be in another line of work, however, think of your current occupation as an interim means to an end, nothing more.

CHALLENGES

Succeeding at a fulfilling job is one of the best means for building up self-esteem. Another way is to overcome a difficult challenge. Some challenges are associated with the type of work you do, and those are always fun to tackle and solve. Other challenges are strictly political. Somebody else may be the villain in your situation, but if you fail to overcome the political challenges that person represents, your self-esteem will suffer because he or she controls your satisfaction not you.

One of the better ways to boost your self-esteem is to look at politics as a challenging game. Consider yourself a player, not a spectator. Give yourself the goal of convincing someone you detest that you are his best friend and have his interests at heart. Although the truth is that you can't stand him, challenge yourself to care about his needs and make him believe that he very much needs you to meet his goals.

Others might advise you to picture him naked so you can see that he is only human, but let's not get gross. I say, think of him as just another human being who, beneath his tough, self-reliant veneer, is fighting for his survival and is just as frightened as you are. Regardless of how strong and independent he may seem, he has needs. If you can find out what they are and help him to meet them, he may not be able to help himself from doing the same for you.

You may never like this game, but you have no choice but to play it. When you examine the world in its essence, everything is about individual survival. Companies are not run to generate profits any more than governments are run to provide for common needs. Most organizations are run for one purpose and one purpose only: to protect the jobs and other interests of the people in charge.

......14......

Don't Let the Bastards Grind You Down

Office politics has only two rules, one of which we've already talked about:

> *To meet your own needs, you must first*
> *meet the needs of others.*

The second rule is:

> *If others don't respond favorably even after considerable*
> *back-scratching on your part, say to hell with them*
> *and write your own rules.*

Keeping both these dictums in mind, don't put up with peers and subordinates who are difficult, antagonistic, or unhelpful even through you have gone to great lengths to motivate them.

Take action against them at the first sign of trouble. Declining to do so would be equivalent to issuing engraved announcements that identify you as a naive pushover.

Before going on the offensive, however, take another look at what motivates an uncooperative person. Have you missed anything? Is he just unresponsive in general, or is the problem merely a function of his personality and how he does things? If an individual is habitually late, for example, you should allow for that by giving him tighter deadlines or longer lead times than anyone else. He may react fast only if he thinks a disaster is imminent. You may have to use more powerful spin for him to properly sense the gravity of your situation. You might become suspicious if someone cried wolf every time he needed help, but that's exactly what you have to do to move some people off dead center.

Tell problem subordinates when you are upset and why. And ask them why they have not been more reliable in complying with your wishes. Restate your expectations, and invite them to voice their problems and their questions. If they do not improve after that, and if you are certain you have scratched their backs appropriately, explain yourself again. On that occasion, however, put them on notice of losing their jobs in a fixed time if they aren't doing what you want. Kick them out if they don't reform.

You can't fire someone who's at the same level you're at, but you can confront him if he has paid little or no attention to your motivations. Don't hurl accusations at him. That will put him on the defensive and cause him to fight back. Name calling would probably follow, and you'd both become madder without resolving a thing. Do yourself a favor. Rather than starting (escalating, if you prefer) a war with this person, be political. Tell him that you assume he has nothing personal against you and that you hope he doesn't think you're mad at him. Say that, as far as you're concerned, he is one of the good guys whose time is too valuable to waste playing political games.

Schmooze and stroke as furiously as you can. Say that you admire him, his work, his office, or even his dumb jokes. Don't tell him you think they're dumb. Tell him you know he is busy, but that his help is desperately needed. Instead of saying that you want him to solve *your* problem, however, position yourself as working on the *boss's* problem. Imply that your boss is already relying on him.* If he wants to know why, stroke. Tell him that he was mentioned as the most qualified individual.

To show a recalcitrant peer how enraged and determined you are, start by getting angry about him within earshot of a crony who will tell him all about your outburst. Don't just fume and explode, and don't get personal. Say calmly—but loudly enough to be overheard—to a friend that this individual has done something (or declined to do something) that interfered with your work and that you have no intention of letting him get away with it again. Will someone back down and turn from a slimeball to a saint just because you mouth off a bit? Maybe not, but people will be less likely to mess with you if they think you are going to fight back.

You may think of trying to get your boss to intercede if someone is giving you a hard time, but tread carefully. To a boss's way of thinking, the problem might be nothing more than your inability to get along with people and solve your own problems. He could be all wrong, but he's the boss; he doesn't have to be right. All he has to do is to focus on his goals. If you block that focus on what he might mistakenly see as a dispute he wants no part of, he's going to get angry—at you, not at that jerk who's causing the problem.

This doesn't mean that you can't go to a boss; it means that

---

*Or his boss, or any higher-level boss.

you have to go the smart way. Plan ahead and be prepared to be specific. Don't spout generalities or tell stories about what happened last week or might happen next year. Address what is happening now, and which of the boss's priorities is in jeopardy. Show how you have done your part, how everything is ready despite what others were supposed to do.

Drop your bomb at that point and show what the problem is. Identify the culprit, but aside from pointing out what wasn't done to help (or what was done to hinder) you, don't say vile things about him. Focus on defining how to overcome the problems he has created. Give the boss a plan for getting back on track.

Document your case. Crank up that memo mill. Find a way to use your adversary as a scapegoat on whom to blame problems. Every time he refuses to help, or throws roadblocks in your way, put the situation on paper in all its gory details. Not only should you describe how his lack of cooperation caused a problem, but also what the problem was or is, where and when it occurred, who else was affected, and how you think the mess can be cleaned up.

Always use your memo mill when you want something from others. Tell them on paper what you want and when you want it. Send a copy to your boss and also to the boss of the person whose help you are seeking. Throw in enough spin so the urgency of your request is clear, and include a statement to the effect that:

> *If I do not hear a response from you to the contrary by August 4, I will assume that this schedule is acceptable to you.*

As a result of someone's failure to be a team player, your plans may be thwarted. If you want to get back on track, absolve yourself of blame, and prevent the same thing from happening again, be ruthless. If someone transgresses, speak to the offending individual and see whether a simple misunderstanding is the guilty party. At the same time, however, write a memo. Make it clear who was at fault for any schedule delays and be sure that person is never you. Add spin that clearly shows you not to be at fault, what took place, and show how more of the same will lead to more problems. Most important, don't just cast blame, recommend a solution and ask for action. Attach a copy of your original memo requesting the help that never came. Send copies to everyone who has even a peripheral connection to the issue.

Then, if you do go to your leader for help, cover one issue at a time, backed up in each instance by a mountain of memo-mill evidence. Even if the problem was sudden and there's only one memo, you're covered. The boss can see that you're not asking him to fight your battles, and also that you're not engaging in general warfare. The perception you want the boss to sense is that you are bringing a problem to his attention, your only concern is in his priorities, and that you have a plan for making certain they are reached.

Difficult bosses are a little trickier than peers or subordinates. Okay, they're a *lot* trickier. To give them no excuses for claiming that you have circumvented their authority, you can and you should use your memo mill to document to your boss what you want and what you're thinking. What you may not be able to do is to use your memos as a club over his head.

One time a boss told me that a brochure I had designed had the ugliest color he had ever seen. He demanded to see my color charts so he could pick out something more to his liking for our next printing. He did, but when we ran out of brochures several months later, I went back to find his notation in the color charts. His choice certainly didn't reflect my taste, but that's what he wanted, so that's what we gave him.

Not fifteen minutes after the new batch arrived in the office, however, he demanded that I tell him the name of the lunatic who picked that awful color. I got great joy out of watching him squirm as I showed him the place where he had initialed our color charts.

Was that the smart thing to do? I thought it was at the time, but not now. He got so upset at me that I thought he was going to have a stroke. He always hated me after that. I could have avoided the whole scene by showing him the color charts again *before* we had the brochures printed, but at the time, I valued my creative independence more than I did my job security.

Memos are great for documenting what is supposed to be done at which time. In the arena of decisions and preferences, however, we sometimes have to be sufficiently creative to realize that some bosses will want the last word today, regardless of what they may have said yesterday.

Be careful with these characters. Since they think from the seat of their pants instead of the top of their heads, their thinking is hard to predict from one day to the next. Holding power over you, they can keep you pinned down if their feathers get too ruffled, and they can kick you out if they feel that you threaten them.

When a boss refuses to respond after you have scratched his back, your gut reaction may be to tell him what he wants to hear, to be the catalyst for making him look foolish, or perhaps even to crush his skull. You can pursue all these tactics, and they may help you feel temporarily better, but none of them will put an extra penny in your pocket, and none is a long-term solution to your career problems. Consider instead the path I've laid out in the balance of this chapter. My plan will help ensure that bosses get no more from you than what they pay you in one form or another. Combined with alternative ways of meeting your needs, the following stratagem can, at the very least, help you feel better about yourself, and possibly also to put some more money in your pocket.

PROTECT YOUR TIME

Aside from your abilities, you are valuable to a boss for only one reason—your willingness to spend time on his behalf. The problem you face is that his boss, his cohorts, your peers, and even your subordinates will also make demands on your time.

Note closely that I said "your" time. As I pointed out in chapter 2, you do not own "your" desk or "your" office. The company owns those things, but *you* own your time, and your time is your life. If you don't own that, what do you own? Your boss *never* gets to possess your time, he merely pays you for the use of it—not all of it, just some.

One way to protect your time is to pull a Greta Garbo and become incommunicado. You probably can't cut yourself off from the boss, but you could be highly selective in answering correspondence and returning phone calls from him as well as from everyone else. If you spend too little time dealing with people, however, you will spend too little time networking with them and scratching their backs. They'll get none of your time, but that's just half the story. Having given them nothing but indifference, that's exactly what you're likely to get from them if you ever need more than a small favor.

I say strike a balance and consider some of your time as an investment you make now in hopes that it will pay soon pay off. However, you can't continue investing if your bosses and co-workers grab your time, your energy, your know-how, and your loyalty, while giving you nothing in return but empty promises and disappointment. If you habitually allow them to take advantage of you, not only will you hate your job, but you won't like yourself a whole lot, either.

Many demanding bosses are charismatic and fun to work with. Some of them are opportunists, not long-range thinkers or good managers. They plan ahead for no more than a few seconds at a time, and sweeping emotions often govern their actions. Workaholism is one of their biggest problems. They live to work. If you take the opposite tack and work to live, reporting to them can be quite chaotic, and rewarding only for its sheer excitement.

Twenty-one years ago, my then boss called me in on the Fourth of July, a paid holiday. I was home with a houseful of friends and family, but that clown was in the office, and he had a problem. It could have waited a day (or even a few days) to be solved, but the way he carried on, you would have thought that the fate of western civilization hung on my fixing that problem immediately.

So, I drove in and helped him out. When I asked several weeks later for two hours off to make up for the time I worked that day, however, he reacted as if I had asked to borrow his blood for several weeks. He told me that I was unprofessional and had a "bad" attitude. What was my offense? Expecting compensation for my work.

The only thing that was bad, however, was my judgment. I shouldn't have gone to the office on a day off. I should have said no, and if he persevered, I should have said that my car had broken down and I couldn't find anyone to fix it on the Fourth of July. I could also have told him that I had to see my brother, who was run over by a car. He never knew that my sister has only one brother.

You might view such thinking as unprofessional, but I don't. I have nothing against professionalism. I'm against only the kind of "professionalism" that demands senseless sacrifices. Many bosses would love you to believe that the true professional aspires only to the satisfaction of being a loyal employee who has done a good job. That is sheer bullfeathers. Satisfaction *can* be derived from work well done, but I can't meet my expenses armed only with that sort of satisfaction. The bank won't accept it as legal tender.

The whole idea of working for a living is to rent your time to an employer in return for satisfaction *as you see it,* not to give it away for less than you want in accordance with some bogus definition of professionalism. Here's a better definition:

> *A professional does something well,*
> *and then gets paid for it—all of it.*

Donate your time to churches or synagogues, to charities, to friends and relatives, and to political or social causes, but not to corporate entities. Invest your time in bosses only if you have a reasonable expectation of getting an acceptable return (monetary or otherwise) for your troubles. Offer up your time for any less than that, and you're either a fool, a masochist, or a big fan of indentured servitude.

SORRY, BUT

You're not exactly shocked that the cheap so-and-so wouldn't budge on his decision to freeze your salary, but you're hurt that he obviously takes you to be an idiot. You'd have to be pretty gullible to believe that preposterous story he gave you about not being able to afford to give you a raise. The company spent a fortune on that stupid sales meeting in Phoenix last month, and that new Mercedes the boss is driving must cost a fortune by itself. Why do they have the money for all that stuff, but not for you? They can't honestly admit to their greed without looking totally lacking in class, so they twist the truth to come up with those laughable "can't afford it" stories. You could question the validity of their position, but not without getting embroiled in an argument you can't possibly win.

If you are convinced that the boss is lying like a rug about being unable to respond adequately to your wish list after you have scratched his back for longer than you care to admit, strike back. Tell him that, to make ends meet financially, you will have to take a second job several nights a week. You might even want to say that you will be taking a third job on weekends. Say that you have no choice. Assure him that the other jobs will not interfere with your work and that he can always count on you to "get the job done."

After that, come in on time every morning, do your work, and continue to scratch that boss's back in every legitimate way but one. Make it a practice to start looking at your watch a few minutes before the end of the official business day. When five o'clock rolls around, *vanish*. I don't care where you go at that time, just go. Don't stay a minute late, and don't you dare come in on weekends.

Make sure everyone is convinced that you're going to a second job or looking for a second job. If your boss asks how the after-hours work is going, tell him "terrible" and ask if he can suggest any remedies.

I'm not telling you to take either a second job or a third job. Whether you can or you do get extra work is up to you. I'm merely suggesting that if you are going to be paid as little as possible, you should do no more than what you have to do. If you need more pay, protect enough time to make more elsewhere.

On the other hand, if the boss asks with whom you're working, nicely tell him that it's not a competitor, but that you've been asked not say who it is. I suggest this response for two reasons. First, it covers you in case you really have no other jobs. Second, it is self-empowering. It gives you time at which the boss can't control you. Make him fall for it and you'll feel great. He may even feel jealous and try to woo you back.

Eventually, he may pressure you to put in late hours one night or to work on a crucial project on a Saturday. Say no. When he insists, tell him you have no choice. Again, ask for his advice on what you can do. If he wants you badly enough, he might even come up with some ideas that would let you quit those jobs he thinks you have.

COMPENSATING

You worked hard on Monday, and you accomplished a lot. But you should have been able to leave twenty minutes earlier than you did. It's not that you love the place so much that you couldn't bear to leave. Rather, the boss

- let that staff meeting drag on an hour longer than necessary.
- failed to finish approving your project plans for a customer until a half hour after the normal courier pickup. Instead of going straight home, now you have to go out of your way to a drop-box so the plans can be delivered to the customer by the next morning.
- was late for a meeting with you because he got sucked into a ridiculously long phone conversation with a friend of his who wouldn't shut up.
- insisted that you finish a proposal today. You know that

the customer is on vacation until Thursday, but that doesn't matter to your boss. He wants you to show him the entire proposal on Monday.

Despite all this, you do on Monday everything you wanted to do that day. The only problem is that you stayed at work twenty minutes longer than you wanted to stay.

Twenty minutes. That doesn't sound like all that much, but think about it. Twenty minutes a day for five days a week adds up to an hour and forty minutes. Over the course of a year, that's fifty-two hundred minutes, or eighty-six hours. That's eleven working days! I'm not saying that you have to limit yourself to a forty-hour week. Eighty-six extra hours a year is a lot, regardless of how much time you'd prefer to work. If you decide to put in a fifty-hour week, eighty-six hours a year is the equivalent of almost nine working days. On top of a sixty-hour week, eighty-six hours is still a lot; seven work days per year.

How long you want to work is up to you. How long you are forced to work beyond that is quite another matter. You were hired to do a job, not to serve a sentence. Your boss sets the agenda for your job. He is the person who establishes what has to be done, and you are the person he has hired to do it. But were you told before you started that you would have to be available all hours of the night and on holidays to make up for his refusal or inability to plan any further ahead than the tip of his nose? Did the job description say anything about foregoing family and friends just so you could grovel to some egomaniac by pandering to his paranoia?

When customers buy products from a store, their purchases are charged on the basis of price. The more they buy, the more they pay. If a customer took six apples and wanted to pay for only five, the store owner would be outraged, and rightfully so. He'd be out of his mind to give away that apple for nothing. One apple might not seem like a lot, but if twenty customers a day wanted the same deal, that store owner would be out the price of fifty-two hundred apples a year. Sound familiar? It adds up.

Your time is valuable. Recognize that value. Twenty minutes a day is no less than a week out of your life every year. Are you willing to give away that much time in return for nothing other than the privilege of keeping your job? I sure hope not.

In enlightened organizations, there is no need to give your time away for nothing. People who put in an extra effort are rewarded with extra pay, recognition, or some other form of compensation. As long as you're happy with what that is, it needn't be monetary. If you're not, I urge you to do some compensating of your own.

If you think that the boss forced you to work twenty minutes too long on Monday because of his lack of consideration, his stupidity, or his poor management, compensate by putting in twenty minutes less than usual as soon as you can do so without adversely affecting your work. It doesn't matter whether that turns out to be twenty minutes on Tuesday or ten minutes each on Wednesday and Friday. What's important is that you keep—and even—the score. If he adds twenty minutes to your load every day, come in late every day or take the extra minutes at lunch or at quitting time.

I used to work at a place where compensating like this was developed into an art form. The boss, whom I'll call John, worked out every morning at a gym, sauntering into the office at about 11 A.M. He stayed until eight or nine at night. That didn't bother me. What bothered me was that he expected the rest of us to stay as late as he did.

Arthur Webster was our sales manager, but I always thought of Art as a maestro. He played John like a Stradivarius. Art never came in before ten in the morning. In mid-afternoon, when John was busy presiding over meetings and fielding phone calls, Art took care of business—personal business. He paid his bills, talked to his wife and friends around the country, and discussed the latest football or baseball results with his office cronies.

Of course Art would work in the afternoon, but mostly after 5:30 or 6. That's when John would start to stroll out into the corridors and offices to peruse his kingdom. Warned by a network of fellow conspirators who also stayed late, Art made sure that John liked what he saw: all work, no bull sessions, and no sign of anyone having gone home. Occasionally, John would call everyone in to his office at 7:30 or so, when he would regale them with stories about how he brilliantly founded the business in the days of yore. Some people found it hard to look excited after the third or fourth retelling, but not Art. He always looked spellbound.

Art and his cohorts may have stayed in the office for eleven to twelve hours a day, but they worked four hours, tops. I came in at nine and worked at least as long as Art, but I had other priorities, so I left at five. That annoyed John. He never complained about my work; not once. But he frequently expressed his disappointment at my missing most of his evening meetings. I'm sure Art Webster never heard complaints like that. He got to be vice president approximately fifteen months before I got to be fired.

BE PROACTIVE

It's Thursday and tonight's big concert has been sold out for weeks. But you have collected on a favor, and now you have a pair of tickets for choice seats. They cost you more than a few bucks, but that's okay. This event is *really* special. Now all you have to do is to leave work on time. That would not usually be a problem, but ten days ago, you started working on a proposal for what would be the biggest contract the company has ever had. Ever since, your boss has been acting like a chicken with its head cut off.

The proposal isn't due until next Monday, and you fully expect to work all weekend on it. On two different occasions in the past week, however, the boss came to you with urgent requests that you stay late to take care of a problem that just *had* to be resolved immediately. In each case, it was nothing that couldn't have been put off until the following morning, but you stayed anyway.

That was okay. You didn't have concert tickets on those days. What are you going to do if he materializes at a quarter to five today with another stupid emergency? Do you wait to see what happens and resign yourself to the possibility of forfeiting the money you spent and not attending the concert just because your idiot boss has a panic attack?

One alternative would be to tell him about your tickets and assure him that you will take care of the problem early the following morning. Logical people would accept that, but this guy doesn't work on logic. Let's assume you have mentioned personal plans to him on previous occasions when he has sought your help. Assume further that he reacted with rage and hysterics about your perceived lack of loyalty.

Or, you could be imaginative, possibly even bold. Say "we" but think "me." That's what the boss is doing. For you to do the same in this instance, you have to be sure that if he does come around just before quitting time, he won't be able to find you.

If you have a customer, supplier, or consultant whom you have to see, for example, make an appointment for 3:30 in the afternoon and leave your office at 3. Do it even earlier if you

can. If that isn't feasible, perhaps there's a meeting you want
to have with someone in a different part of the building. You
can leave to see that person at 4, finish at 5, and then exit out
a side door. Can't do that either? How about coming in an
hour early in the morning and leaving at 4?

These suggestions are relatively benign, but more drastic
measures are available. I know people who have called in sick
or left work with alleged toothaches or other ailments, just to
be sure that work did not interfere with their personal plans.
Others have had their wives or husbands call in with news of
some disaster such as burst plumbing.

All the last-minute crises that are thrust upon you at work
might be avoided if the boss had a little consideration and did
a little planning, but that may never happen. The last thing on
the minds of most bosses is consideration for anyone but
themselves. They move through their careers by sheer force of
will, not by planning. They're not going to change their ways,
and you probably will not be able to force them to change.
What you can do is accept them as they are and be more
aggressive in protecting your time from them.

Let's consider another example. You're a salesperson whose
territory is the state of California. You were thinking of taking a vacation day Friday and then spending a long weekend
on a friend's boat in San Diego. Then the boss calls. His office
is in New York. He asks you to call on some accounts in the
San Francisco area next Thursday and Friday so you can show
them the company's new fall line. Did I say "asks"? A more
accurate verb would be "demands." He says that if you don't
arrive before your competition does, you'll lose the business
and then your job.

That really frosts you. He's never even met these customers. You know them well. They've been buying from you for
more than ten years. You don't take them for granted. They
wouldn't turn down a good opportunity to save money if they

could beat your prices, but one call from you on Thursday and they would at least hold off until you could get to them on Monday. No harm would be done by delaying the San Francisco trip by three days, but this boss wouldn't see it that way. He'd get all steamed up and accuse you of not paying enough attention to your responsibilities to the company.

Fed up with his micromanaging your work and getting upset over nothing, you're determined not to let him screw up your life anymore. That's when you remember what one of your customers said a few weeks ago about a series of new products another one of your competitors has introduced. You don't think it is anything to worry about, but the boss doesn't have to know that.

Tell him you were alarmed to hear about these products. Spin your story so the problem sounds so grave that they have to be your top priority. Say that you want to see them for yourself so you can intelligently respond to the threat they represent. Where can you view these little gems? You guessed it—San Diego. So you'll have to take an hour to look at them. Maybe you can do that Thursday night, but that's another fact the boss's ego does not have to be burdened with. Just don't forget to confirm to him that you'll call San Francisco on Thursday and go there on Monday.

I do not like going to the lengths described here. Nor do I suggest making a habit of avoiding every unpleasant assignment that comes your way, or being out of sight each time management comes calling. I urge only that you protect your interests and your priorities by first protecting your time from needless encroachment by thoughtless bosses.

LINES IN THE SAND

When I was an engineering manager in St. Louis, the company sales manager was Paul Nelson, who was always jockeying for position and perpetually looking for ways to make himself look good. One year he thought that one of our new products had such huge potential that it would be his ticket to fame and fortune. Paul drew up grand sales promotion plans, but I wasn't happy with them. He wanted to start right away, but I didn't think the product was far enough along in its safety testing to be ready for general sales. We could get it ready, but that would take another eight months to a year.

Our boss didn't take sides. He said only that we should put off any decisions. Paul agreed if my people promised to move things along as quickly as possible, and I said we would. I also volunteered to keep him up to date with everything that happened. After that, I went out of my way to communicate with Paul. I called him whenever we had progress or setbacks, and I invited him to sit in on our testing and our staff meetings. I even invited him to give us his ideas.

That was a mistake. He soon began to make design suggestions. His ideas weren't particularly good, but he wasn't concerned with good; he was driven by greed. This became a problem when he started to dominate our staff meetings with his questions, to waste our time with proposals that wouldn't work, and to insist that we take certain shortcuts in the product development process. We were trying our best to come up with a product that was safe and sellable, but his badgering was beginning to get in our way.

It was also annoying, but I let it pass until he accused me of deliberately slowing things down. Then he questioned my judgment. I would have preferred to ignore him at that point, but several times a day he was in our hair, demanding to know why we weren't working in closer accordance with his wishes. That did it. Weekly progress reports were one thing, but I wasn't about to answer to him hourly. Fed up with his insults as well as his interference, I took Paul aside and told him to cut out the crap right then and there. I said that I would continue to keep him up to date on the status of our work, and that I would even continue to listen to any constructive views he had. I would not, however, listen to any more of his complaints, demands, or insults. If he didn't like that, I went on, he could take them up with my boss. Did that shut him up? You bet it did. I was probably not one of his favorite people after that, but then he never did get in my way again.

With some antagonists in some situations, all the back-scratching in the world won't help. They either can't or won't give you satisfaction no matter what you do. They have too much ego or too much fear to do anything else but be contrary. It doesn't matter that you have no intention of hurting them. They're frightened—perhaps paranoid—and they probably don't know any other way of relating to you. The longer you have to deal with people like this, the more you'll come to hate what they are doing (or trying to do) to you. You'll feel as if you're sitting on an imaginary fence that you're straddling as you compensate and compromise to make the best of things.

The problem is, if you hate a situation long enough, you'll sooner or later fall off that fence. That's when you will have reached your "line in the sand," a point beyond which you will have an uncontrollable urge for immediate satisfaction. That's the point at which you'll feel absolutely compelled to take action no matter what the consequences.

This may mean going out on a limb if you are dealing with a boss whose only way of interfacing with people is to attack. If your relationship has already deteriorated to the point at which it has become destructive, on the other hand, you may have little to lose. When a job ties your stomach in knots and leaves you with a headache that never goes away, you may have something to gain by forcing the issue. Is the job worth the extent to which it is tearing you apart? You tell me. I don't know what your boiling point is.

What I *do* know is that if you appear angry enough and yell loudly enough, a bully will probably back down. Unless they are psychopathic, bullies usually do back down when confronted by an opponent rather than a doormat. Their power over you is fueled by your propensity to cringe. If you assertively show them your claws, they often turn tail.

Sometimes, they'll back down after seeing that you refuse to roll over and play dead just because they make noise. One boss who wanted me out threatened to put certain comments about me in my records unless I resigned. I knew what his game was. I could collect unemployment compensation only if he fired me, not if I resigned. I needed that money, so I played my own game. *"What records?"* I asked. *"Who's going to see them?"* Exploding with indignation, I made up my mind that if he forced me out, he would pay a painful price. Realizing that he might be blustering his way into a slander suit, he quickly reversed course. We parted, but on terms that were acceptable to both of us.*

Please understand that drawing your line in the sand does *not* have to mean waiting until your job is on the line or putting it there prematurely. There's no need to be reckless or stupid. You may be able to cross your line, accomplish your goal, and cross back without getting hurt. All you need do is to avoid sticking your foot in your mouth when you open it. This isn't hard. Just focus on your goals, think diplomacy, and remember to take your stands on principle rather than on confrontation or brinkmanship.

*By the way, I checked. The liar gave me fabulous references.

That's what Noah Billings did. Noah had a master of science degree in computer engineering. Armed with the latest know-how of the digital age, he took a job with a research laboratory whose manager asked him to help out in some building renovations just under the roof of the single-story building they worked in.

Before he knew what was happening, Noah found himself in old clothes and sneakers, negotiating through a crawl space to lay down insulation above the ceiling of his office. There was no light up there except one Noah carried with him. Wires were all over the place, it was filthy, and the temperature was intolerably high. If he missed a beam, as he did several times, he put his foot right through the plaster ceiling. He was afraid of falling through and he hated being up there, yet he did not like saying no. After a couple of days, however, that's exactly what he said.

"Whaddya mean, you won't do this anymore?" roared the boss. Noah calmly explained himself. He said he could deal with the danger, but that he hadn't studied computer engineering for six years to crawl through dirt in the dark and the heat.

Noah reached his line in the sand, recognized it, crossed it constructively, and crossed back. He also got his way. Someone else finished the work above the ceiling. Noah didn't get fired. He got the respect and friendship of his boss, and he also got to keep his job.

WHEN ALL ELSE IS SAID AND DONE

You may have a lousy job, but in no way are you stuck there. If a job is *that* bad and upsetting you *that* much for *that* long, and if additional back-scratching proves to be fruitless, maybe you *should* cross your line in the sand and walk out. At the least, you should dramatically increase your efforts to find another job. A good rule of thumb in this regard is that if you think you're doing all you can to sell your services to other employers, double your efforts. You might not get the ideal replacement job before you go, but you could very well come up with something that is less awful; not what you want, but better than what you've got. Such a job may be temporary, but what job isn't?

Presuming that you must make a move, do it at a time (and in a manner) of *your* choosing, not your boss's. Once you cross your line emotionally, it may be impossible to cross back. If you hang around after deciding that you hate the place, your attitude will sour and your output will plummet. Bosses draw their own lines. Stop doing your work and they're the ones who will act. You may not meet your goals just by doing your work to perfection, but you definitely can get stifled or sacked by doing it poorly or not at all.

This is the pickle in which many people find themselves. But instead of taking a gaze-at-the-sky approach and coming up with interim solutions that make the best of their bad situations, many of them do nothing except waste time feeling sorry for themselves. Instead of drawing a line in the sand, they bury their heads in it.

Abandoning all rational thought, they embrace the brilliant notion that they could improve their lives by endlessly commiserating with their co-workers and bad-mouthing their bosses, the economy, inept subordinates, jealous peers, the government, and other scapegoats. Clueless as to the futility of this "strategy," they are so busy whining that they have no time to do anything that would actually improve their lives.

Some people may have picked you up or helped you out occasionally, but they can't spend all their time taking care of you. They have their own jobs to worry about. Still others may have set you up, let you down, or done you in, but the most they are guilty of is having caused some of your problems. You can't blame them if those problems never go away. You can, but you'd be wrong.

If you doubt me, look around. Your arms and legs aren't moved by pulling strings. Examine your wrists and ankles. They're not in chains. Look down. Your brain might be mired in cement, but your feet certainly aren't. Lastly, inspect your clothes. If you don't see footprints, you are probably not a doormat. Stop acting like one. It might not be easy, but at any time of your choosing, you can pick yourself up, dust yourself off, and move on to a better place politically and emotionally, if not geographically or financially.

When you need to improve your life, there is just one person you can count on to make things happen. Like it or not, that person is you. So don't just sit there and bitch about your job. Set your focus, follow your dreams, get political, observe, test, scratch backs, motivate, and *do* something about it!

.....AFTERWORD.....

People who know me will probably be surprised to hear that I'm telling you to make politics the cornerstone of your career. They know how much I hate the usual brand of back-stabbing office politics and everything it stands for. This is the beauty of the back-scratching technique described on the preceding pages. Without making you stoop to the gutter, it gives you a powerful way to motivate bosses and others to take good care of you—not in spite of their selfishness, because of it. I'd rather have job satisfaction attainable without any kind of politics, but we must deal with things as they are, not with how they should be or could be in a perfect world.

Don't use back-scratching only at work; make it the focal point of your life. Avoid being a doormat, identify your goals, focus on nothing else, know how far you can be pushed before drawing a line in the sand, have a good Plan B, scratch as hard as you can without gouging or being gouged, and don't expect overnight results. Motivating others to help you is infinitely more productive than doing everything by yourself, but you must have patience.

Having said all that, I guess I had better follow my own advice. I certainly didn't do everything that had to be done to get this book published. Stuart Krichevsky worked with me for months to flush out the concepts you see here. Stuart is more than an agent, he's a great sounding board. I also like to think that he's a friend.

After Stuart sold the book, I wrote it, but not without more help. Editor Matt Walker read my drafts and showed me how to fix them where they were broken. My thanks to Matt for his many excellent ideas. Most of them I used. I thank him also for the few I vetoed. For me to accept all of his suggestions would have been entirely out of character, so I exercised a few prerogatives solely on principle.

The most gratitude goes to my wife, Eileen. Every time I write a book, I promise her that it won't consume my every spare moment, and yet every time it does. Why she puts up with me, I'll never know.

Wesley Hills, New York

March 1997